Off the Fence

Live the Life You Were Born to Live

David Kinnan

renownpublishing

Love - Give - Go!

Renown Publishing
www.renownpublishing.com

Off the Fence / David Kinnan
ISBN: 978-0-578-92731-2

If you want to know what a heart fully committed to Jesus looks like in real-world terms, this book is for you. Dave Kinnan tackles the question and answers with a helpful and practical look at what it means to live a life of Love, Generosity, and focused Mission.

Larry Osborne

Author and Pastor, North Coast Church

I love when a book meets you right where you are and brings you somewhere special. That is exactly what this book does. With honesty and vulnerability, David brings us straight from the Bible to street level, where we live. This journey with Jesus is too important to be lived on autopilot. This book is a gift to help ignite a much-needed fire in our hearts.

Daniel Fusco

Pastor at Crossroads Community Church (Vancouver, WA), Author of *Crazy Happy*, TV & Radio Host

Off the Fence ... a book for honest Christ-seekers. Filled with hope. David is personally transparent and authentic, along with strong biblical examples of a God who loves unconditionally. I can only imagine the radical transformation a city and beyond would experience if people moved "off the fence." Take the challenge! God is waiting!

Jo Anne Lyon

General Superintendent Emerita of The Wesleyan Church

Many of us know what it is like to be on the sideline wanting to be in the game. Even more of us know what it is like to allow procrastination to cause us to miss an amazing ministry opportunity. This is why Pastor David Kinnan's new book, *Off the Fence*, is so important. For nearly a decade, I have watched as this exceptional

leader jumped off the fence and grew a world-impacting ministry. My prayer is that all who read this book will receive the necessary nudge to jump off the fence into their own world-impacting journey.
Joseph Sangl
President & CEO, INJOY Stewardship Solutions and Founder, I Was Broke. Now I'm Not.

As he's done for years in the pastorate, so many times in this book David does it again. He's given us a read that will transform the lukewarm believer to what Mama called an "on fire" Christian. Our Christian light can easily be dampened given the problems that surround us. But David delivers, here, an accessible and practical guide that helps us live authentically as believers who refuse to allow this cold world to affect the impact of our faith. No matter where you may be in your spiritual journey, read this book. Let David remind you of the fundamentals of our Christian faith that will inspire any reader to make the jump from cold to hot, dead to alive, and hopeless to hopeful!
Ricky Jenkins
Senior Pastor, Southwest Church

"There is so very much God desires to do for us. But we limit him if we will not "get off the fence." That's our part. And that is why you want to read this book. David Kinnan offers an honest, inspiring, accessible, and culturally practical guide to real faith. From the truth of the Bible to life stories, you'll know precisely what to do next. So, get some friends or a small group and make this a priority. The things that limit your life are on the other side of the fence!
Kevin Myers
Senior Pastor, 12Stone Church

David Kinnan is one of the most intentional pastors I know. His life is devoted to helping pave the way for others to know what it looks like to live fully for God. David knows that none of us get to a healthy place in life on accident, so in this book, he shows us the path we need to intentionally follow to do a checkup on ourselves and evaluate our spiritual health. I invite you to get "off the fence" and see where the path leads you.

Craig A. Dunn
CEO of Wesleyan Investment Foundation

To my bride, Katy.
This book isn't for you—it's because of you.
You say, "Yes," when most say, "No."
These words are our *words.*
I'm the luckiest.

CONTENTS

Yoga Pants and Fried Chicken

Athleisure. What a weird word. In print, it doesn't even look like a real word, but it's legit. Officially placed in the Merriam-Webster dictionary, athleisure is "casual clothing designed to be worn both for exercising and for general use." You might know it best as the yoga-pants trend. Beginning around 2009, the market for this type of apparel began to climb. It created what *Business Insider* magazine called the "Denim Apocalypse."[1]

The trend to wear workout clothes to work has many possible explanations—comfort being an obvious one. Marshal Cohen, chief apparel analyst for the market-research firm NPD Group said, "The clothes are comfortable and suit a fitness-conscious lifestyle." However, an interesting statistic provides a telling detail: the number of people buying yoga pants didn't correspond with the number of people actually doing yoga. Experts (and probably you and I) seem to agree we now dress in a way that corresponds with how we *expect to live*. More directly, we might not work out, but we'll dress like we do.

Full disclosure: at times, I've used the same approach with my relationship with God. Except, rather than enjoying a thriving relationship with my Creator, I found I only "looked the part." Instead of experiencing peace, joy, challenge, or any feeling of connection with God, I landed in a comfortable relationship with Him, one that was shallow and self-centered.

This wasn't what I wanted, and it's not what God has invited us to. It's natural to want a thriving relationship with God. Actual conversations with God, hearing what He has to say, experiencing Him here on earth—I think all Christians want that to happen. We don't just want life to have meaning; we want to feel it, experience it, and live it out daily. We want a thriving relationship with God.

When we're in a relationship deficit, one that just isn't meeting our expectations, we begin to be on the lookout for the next something—maybe an emotional experience to fill the emptiness in our heart. Maybe we bridge the gap with a quick Amazon order. Possibly a cookie would help? What about a quick dopamine boost by getting some likes from a social media post? This is what we do: we compensate for what we lack. If you're a Christian, and your relationship with God starts to "lack," don't settle for that.

A relationship with God that once started hotter than a microwaved bowl of oatmeal can soon become like a gallon of milk left out of the fridge—lukewarm, at best. We like Jesus and honestly want to commit to Him, but easily find ourselves lacking that intensity or connection we had at the beginning.

Does your life reflect Christ and how He taught us to live? Do you want it to? I believe you do. Most people don't read a book called *Off the Fence* if getting off the fence is of zero interest. I bet you've rooted for people who post a pic about their baptism or a verse from the Bible that really spoke to them. I'm sure you've even watched God move in other people's lives. I'm confident you want a real relationship with your Savior. No pretense. No fake-it-till-you-make-it. Let me say it for us all: a genuine, connected relationship with God is available to you and me, this side of heaven.

The relationship we want with God has a responsibility connected to it. Relationships don't thrive if one person just sits on the fence. Long-term sitting breeds apathy. We become lethargic, waiting for God to give us a turn rather than realizing our name has been called. Expecting God to do all the work is a dangerous and spiritually impoverished way to live, and it's not what Jesus intended for us when He came to give us a full life (John 10:10 NIV).

No one truly wants to be an on-the-fence Christian. Talk about unfulfilling! Yet sometimes that's exactly where we find ourselves. Please know I am not here to condemn you if you are struggling in this area. If anyone knows what it's like to struggle with apathy, it's me. You are not alone in this. I've been where you are, and sometimes I still circle back around to those spaces of indifference! But every time, God comes for me and draws me back with His love. I'm here to remind you God is right there—choosing you, calling you, wanting you! I'm just a messenger, encouraging you to embrace the richness of an authentic relationship with Jesus and experience the fruits of that in your life.

A Spiritual Checkup

To break free from the bonds of lukewarm faith—to get off the fence—we need to restore our spiritual health and take personal responsibility for our relationship with God.

The first step is to examine the condition of your spiritual heart. Is it healthy and clean? Has sin—oh, let's get specific—has bitterness or greed been clogging your heart and setting you up for a spiritual heart attack? Did the hurt you experienced put you on the fence (or maybe at rock bottom)? Unhealthy marriage? Bad church experience? Got overlooked by someone? There's a long, long list we can make of the reasons we slowly climbed the fence, sat down, and have been waiting.

In the first three chapters of this book, you'll learn what a healthy spiritual heart looks like and how you can have one yourself. We'll take an in-depth look at the Parable of the Prodigal Son and how it reveals the three main characteristics of a healthy spiritual heart: unconditional love, irrational generosity, and a sense of unwavering mission.

The remaining four chapters focus on how you can maintain the health of your spiritual heart by making sure your relationship with Jesus is authentic and biblically sound.

This begins with learning to experience God as more than just our rescuer and making the effort to show up for Him and for others.

We then continue to mature in our relationship with Jesus by understanding what it means to follow Him. We learn how to take care of our own soul and how to help others experience the same. Your future (or current) marriage needs your soul to be healthy. Your kids (or future kids) have more opportunity to thrive if your soul is healthy. This book will help you get equipped to live a generous, sacrificial life that focuses on rescuing other people and leading them to faith in Christ.

Workbook sections at the end of each chapter will encourage you, with reflection questions and action steps, to experience God for yourself. As you experience more of God, you can then share the hope you have in Christ with other people.

All this adds up to us getting off the fence of being a lukewarm Christian. There is a life available to you where each day becomes an opportunity to experience God—and help others encounter Him as well!

Change Starts with You

Recently, I adjusted my eating habits. Since I was a kid, I have enjoyed food—and lots of it! Donuts. Fried chicken. Fried cheese. Fried onions. Fried anything. Throughout life, and due to the scale telling me bad news, I've attempted different eating tricks and diets. At times, I've blamed my metabolism. I've blamed stress. I've blamed our kids not eating all their food, so Dad obviously needed to clear their plate. We can't waste this stuff, right?

In high school, I was dumped by girls on multiple occasions. That seemed like a viable excuse to eat a Double

Whopper and fries. I've blamed hurt. I've blamed past experiences of being told I needed to eat a lot because I was "a growing boy." You know what changed things for me? You know how I started making wiser eating choices? I personally took on the responsibility of thinking about what I eat, rather than relying on random fly-by diets or past experiences with other people. I told people that I was in "training"—I was learning how to eat the food I should eat in the portions that are appropriate.

A word of caution: it can be tempting for us to blame others for our spiritual condition. *If only* we had a better church, a better pastor, a better Bible study group, we think we would be better Christians!

Whatever your reasons are for your current condition, change needs to start with the individual. The only way for us to not fake this whole thing is to take responsibility for our own lives, determine the changes we desperately need to make, and then make them. We have to choose to get off the fence.

And when we focus on our own issues first, something amazing happens. As each of us works toward becoming a better "me," we will see our church, our workplace, our family start to change. I've applied the content in this book to my marriage, to being a dad, to being a friend, and in how I lead our church. It is life-giving truth that generates so much good. It starts with you. Being a better "me" creates a better "we."

It is my prayer that this book will jostle some things in your life, spurring you into training—training to be a fully devoted follower of Jesus Christ. Maybe a fire in your soul will be lit, one that will change you and the world around you. Maybe it will be the final, *gentle* push you need to get off the fence once and for all. I believe you were born with a longing to be in a relationship with God that is personal and meaningful. Jesus has changed my life. This is His intention with you. Once you connect some initiative to your intentions, you'll never want any other version of life again.

CHAPTER ONE

Love Runs

I get a little worked up about visiting the doctor. It might have something to do with the fact that when I was little, I was afraid of getting shots. I realize most people don't thoroughly enjoy getting shots, but I'd get especially amped up about it in my head. Before a trip to Africa, when I was in the seventh grade, my family and I went to the doctor to get our yellow fever shots. After I got mine, we were standing in the lobby talking and all of my pre-shot nervousness and adrenaline kicked in. Long story short, I passed out. Shots scared me.

Whenever I had a doctor's appointment, I would ask my parents if I was going to get a shot. They would always say they weren't sure. That's parent talk for, "Don't get all worked up and create a scene."

I'm a parent now. My kids ask me the same question about shots because they enjoy going to the doctor about as much as I do. I find myself in that same dilemma, and I wonder if I should change the subject or maybe mention that "shots aren't bad at all." I'm a professional with the distraction tactic—"Hey, there's candy afterward!"—but really, there's no good way to deal with shots. The stress of going to a doctor's appointment and not knowing if there's going to be an unexpected shot still makes my heart race.

Why the talk about the shots? When I go to a doctor, my heartrate is one of the first things that gets checked. The problem with that is, I still show up with my childhood nerves, thinking I'll find a tray of shots sitting next to the exam table—each being a giant steel syringe like you see in scary movies. They know me so well now, I always get my blood pressure checked twice. Every time. And every time, after I see there aren't any clowns with giant syringes, my blood pressure goes down.

If you get injured in a car accident and an ambulance is called to the scene, the medical personnel will, without a doubt, check your vital signs. I guarantee you they will check your heartrate.

Your heart might just be the most important organ in your body, and your heartbeat says a lot about your health. It's a big deal. And it's not just about whether it's beating—it's about how it's beating. Is it in rhythm? Is it functioning the way it's supposed to? The health of your heart is important for your survival! Every thirty-four seconds, someone in the United States dies from heart disease.[2] It's still the number one cause of death in America.

Wise people pay a lot of attention to the condition of their heart. They don't eat donuts every day, they learn to bypass the plate of cookies someone brought in, they tell their waiter no when offered more bread, and they prioritize exercise like their life depends on it. I say "they" because I'm still a work-in-progress when it comes to making these wise choices.

My point isn't to judge how big your steak is or scare you into scheduling an appointment with your doctor. (Although it's never a bad idea to make sure you're in good health.) As important as your physical health is, especially your heart, a healthy spiritual heartbeat should demand your constant attention.

Defining the Spiritual Heart

The phrase *spiritual heart* can get a little confusing. This is the heart that gets broken when people hurt our feelings or mistreat us. If you've ever had a broken heart, you don't forget that pain.

This is the heart going out to people who are lost, hurting, or in need. This is the heart causing you to passionately pour into your work or another endeavor— the heart that makes others say, "Wow! Your heart's really in this!"

Again, though our physical heart is important, our spiritual heart is even more so. Proverbs 4:23 gives us this command: "Above all else, guard your heart, for everything you do flows from it" (NIV).

Those words "above all else" make it clear that guarding our spiritual heart is not something we can afford to neglect. Our spiritual heart is the source of everything we do! It is the source of the decisions we make, the people we choose to date, the effort we put in at work or school, how we spend our time, and what we choose to do or not do with our lives.

If your spiritual heart is not healthy, it doesn't just affect you. It means your integrity is paper-thin. It means you're super-vulnerable to making really dumb decisions. Other people around you are in danger because you will treat them poorly.

In Luke 6:45, Jesus explained: "A good person produces good things from the treasury of a good heart, and an evil person produces evil things from the treasury of an evil heart. What you say flows from what is in your heart" (NLT).

If our spiritual heart is healthy, we will do good things that are pleasing to God. We will treat other people well and do what should be done. Wouldn't you agree? Personally, on days when my heart is healthy, I tend to see others' needs more easily. I find myself pausing to enjoy the simple things or noticing the beauty around me with a heart of thanksgiving toward God. I would even say the voice of God is much clearer when my heart is clean.

Jesus wants us to live full lives in which we thrive spiritually. He said in John 10:10, "The thief comes only to steal and kill and destroy; I have come that they may have life, and have it to the full" (NIV). The thief mentioned in this verse is the devil, the enemy of our souls. He wants to take your heart and make it so toxic, it destroys you and everyone around you.

The full life Jesus desires for us, which He came to bring to us, requires a healthy spiritual heart. Once again, having a healthy spiritual heart is even more important than having a healthy physical heart. Even though you may not be able to see your spiritual heart, you'd better believe it's the most real part of you. Its health will reveal itself in your physical life in obvious ways.

For example, maybe you're single right now but you think you might like to be married someday. You have an idea of some of the traits you'd like your spouse to have. Maybe you even have someone in mind. Either way, you know beyond a shadow of a doubt, you want your future marriage to be awesome. If you want that, you need a healthy spiritual heart. The best marriages aren't because of an ingenious algorithm on a dating website. Thriving marriages happen because of healthy hearts.

How about the job? For a lot of us, work gets a ton of our time. It's natural to have work-related goals and aspirations. The Bible says we should work. Maybe you want to lead a team of people and own a company. I know many business owners utilizing their jobs to make a lasting impact in this world. If that's you—if you have dreams for your life about the kind of work you want to do and the impact you want to have on people—you need to have a healthy spiritual heart. Otherwise, the pressure inevitable at any job makes it easy to let that job run our lives and damage what and who we love the most.

How about kids? We have four kids, and each is uniquely different. Having children is about more than adding to your family or your hopes for some sort of legacy. Children will be impacted by our spiritual state. My health impacts the health of my children. The best parents have healthy spiritual hearts.

Life isn't completely complicated: The health of your spiritual heart determines the quality and direction of your own life and how your life impacts the lives of others.

A Clean Heart

As Christians who desire to grow in our relationship with God and embrace the full life He has for us, our prayer should echo that of the psalmist: "Create in me a clean heart, O God. Renew a loyal spirit within me" (Psalm 51:10 NIV).

Something in us craves that fresh, clean feeling. It's the reason we feel so relieved after we get our car washed, reorganize our closets, or power-wash anything—wow, that's so satisfying! It is the reason showers leave us feeling restored and rejuvenated. There is something about having things in our lives clean and in order that is refreshing. It sets us at ease and really lets us melt into a sense of peace.

I believe our world can be better, but it needs more people with clean hearts. That starts with asking God for His help. And I love how this concept of a "clean heart" makes sense both physically and spiritually. If anything gets into your physical heart—a blood clot, for example—the results could be catastrophic. The same is true for your spiritual heart. If it gets clogged with sin—words and actions displeasing or dishonoring to God—it will affect your decisions. You will deceive people. You will mistreat people. You will lose your way, and you will sabotage your own life.

We tend to struggle in this area, don't we? Not only do we wrestle with our love for God, but we also wrestle with our love for others. Loyalty is not easy for us, especially when relationships get tough.

We cannot keep our hearts clean on our own. To keep your physical heart clean, a doctor will tell you to exercise, stay away from smoking, and eat your vegetables. In my case, the next time I have a doctor's appointment, they might actually show me pictures of vegetables just to confirm I understand what my doctor is recommending.

I'm sure by now you get the point that our spiritual heart is important. It can get dangerously unhealthy, and this can impact our life and the lives of those we love most. I sense you wanting me to move on right now. Lets do it: what does a clean spiritual heart look like?

Thankfully, God has not left us on our own! In fact, we have very specific guidance, straight from God, on how to live this out. We don't have to play guessing games. Jesus' explanation of what a clean spiritual heart looks like can be found in a story He told in Luke 15.

Stories are one of the best vehicles for truth. Whenever Jesus told a story, He was communicating something significant and worth remembering. Let's pay attention then! This story is best known as the Parable of the Prodigal Son:

Jesus continued: "There was a man who had two sons. The younger one said to his father, 'Father, give me my share of the estate.' So he divided his property between them. Not long after that, the younger son got together all he had, set off for a distant country and there squandered his wealth in wild living. After he had spent everything, there was a

*severe famine in that whole country, and he began to be in
need. So he went and hired himself out to a citizen of that
country, who sent him to his fields to feed pigs. He longed
to fill his stomach with the pods that the pigs were eating,
but no one gave him anything. When he came to his senses,
he said, 'How many of my father's hired servants have food
to spare, and here I am starving to death! I will set out and
go back to my father and say to him: Father, I have sinned
against heaven and against you. I am no longer worthy to
be called your son; make me like one of your hired servants.'"*

—Luke 15:11–19 *(NIV)*

The son realized his reckless and irresponsible behavior was not only a sin against his father, who had
generously given him what he asked for, but also a sin
against God. He was ashamed of what he had done, and
he knew he had damaged his relationship with his father.

When we make bad choices, we're tempted to allow
the shame that comes with them to have free access to our
lives. Like the son, we don't believe there will be forgiveness or restoration because we know we don't deserve
it. We feel like the best we can hope for is mercy extended
out of pity. But Jesus didn't end the story there.

Now we get to the lesson in this story, the part where
we really start to grab hold of what it takes to have a
healthy spiritual heart. This next verse shows us a glimpse
of what following Jesus is all about.

*So he got up and went to his father. But while he was still
a long way off, his father saw him and was filled with compassion for him; he ran to his son, threw his arms around
him and kissed him.*

—Luke 15:20 *(NIV)*

We may be tempted to think we would respond like the father in this situation, but reflect on how you last responded to someone who offended you or hurt you. Our response might give us the most honest assessment of how the father's response to his son compares to the posture of our own hearts. It may reveal a behavior for you and me to correct in our own lives.

Full disclosure: it's not natural for me to embrace someone who has hurt me. Most of us don't feel like forgiveness as soon as forgiveness is needed. Do you ever have those debates and conversations in your head? The ones where you tell that person off? Yeah, me neither—I totally don't have a pretend argument in my head where I do all the talking, debating them into a corner with perfectly articulated points of how I'm right and they're wrong, leading them to declare they will change their ways and thank me for such a passionate verbal butt-whooping. Okay, so, I do that. That was a confession.

When I think about how I would feel if I were the father in the story of the prodigal son, the picture in my head is like an old western movie. I'm sitting on my rocking chair on the front porch. Everything is a dull shade of brown. I've got the coolest cowboy hat on and a cheap cigar sitting between my fingers (don't judge—it's a western, remember!). I see my boy walking toward me—the one who dragged our family name through the mud. The boy who showed me my money was more important to him than my relationship with him. It's not my instinct to run to him with open arms, welcome him home, and throw him a party. If I'm real, my heart is cold and ready for a duel.

The last time someone betrayed or hurt you, was your heart filled with compassion, or was it filled with anger and bitterness and plots for revenge? When we're wronged, love is often the furthest thing from our minds.

Jesus made an intentional narrative choice here to have the father run to his son. He could have had the son show up at the house and knock on the door and ask to see his father, or like my western movie idea, Jesus could have said they stared each other down for a while, eyes full of judgment and pain. So, why did Jesus choose to have the father see his son in the distance and run to meet him?

Many theologians believe the father in this story represents God.[3] Interestingly, this is the only place in the Bible where we see God being in a hurry. And why did God the Father run to meet his wayward son? It wasn't simply because He missed him. It was to save him!

Because the son had sinned against God and against his family by demanding his inheritance and completely misusing it,[4] the villagers who saw him return might have cut him off and rejected him from the community. They might have beaten him, publicly humiliated him, or even stoned him to death.

The only way for the son to avoid rejection, public shame, and possible death, and to be received back into the family, was for the father, as the head of the family, to intervene. Knowing his son was vulnerable and in danger while he was still out on the open road, not yet within the safety of the home, the father ran to him to save his life.

If you haven't already traded your yoga pants or sweatpants for a long robe, you may not know what's actually playing out in this story—the significance of the dad running to his son. In order to run, you have to lift up the skirts of the robe and expose your legs.

Let's just stop here for a second. I'm going to bring up the brutal reality of this man's legs. I'm guessing he didn't moisturize. I'm certain he hadn't been sitting out at the pool all summer getting a nice tan. I'm confident this dad's legs weren't in their prime. To add to that, at this time in history and culture, it wasn't particularly dignified to hike up your robe and run. Let's just say, some onlookers would've whispered to others, "Um, *awkward!*"

And yet, the father disregarded what others thought and exposed himself to public shame so he could get to his son. He did this to protect him and bring him back into the family, where he would be safe and forgiven. As a dad, I get this. In my teens and twenties, I still cared about being cool. Once I had kids I was in charge of, cool wasn't cool anymore. Protecting them was cool. Loving them was cool. Supporting my kids was cool. No longer does any liability or social rejection keep me from being present and available to my kids, no matter what they've done with their lives, good or bad. I understand why a dad would disregard the opinions of others in order to meet the needs of his own kid.

I feel like that kind of parental, unconditional love was what motivated the father to behave this way. This is the point of Jesus' story. As a dad, I know the love I have for my kids is a love God has asked me to give to others as well. Unconditional love is a defining characteristic of a clean spiritual heart.

The Cure for Cancel Culture

We live in a culture that mostly offers conditional love. As long as we don't hurt other people, they give us love. If we do hurt them, they show us the door. Our differences are getting gasoline poured on them. Our relationships seem to have weak seams we never knew existed.

I ask a lot of people about the fragility of their friendships, and I usually get a recurring answer. Most of us have multiple friendships seemingly one mistake away from ending. We know for a fact that if we mess up one more time, it's over.

Even though marriage vows directly state *nothing* will end the marriage, I've counseled multiple couples who go into marriage with a long list of deal-breakers. If their spouse does this or doesn't do that, it's over.

Even when we go beyond our personal relationships, it's impossible to escape this conditional love. Our society is shaped by social media and a 24/7 news cycle. Racism and violence dominate the headlines. The news leverages people's fears, and rather than simply providing factual information about the events of the day, they end up helping sever relationships between neighbors. People destroy each other on social media over politics and pronouns, and children are regularly bullied online.

I think we'd all agree we need more love in our lives, but how we do this needs some attention. Maybe we don't need more love—how about fewer conditions? Some of the people who claim to be the most loving are leading the charge to ruin the lives of those who disagree with them. In a pursuit to advocate for a victim, I wonder if we're unintentionally creating more victims because our love is so conditional.

The health of your love—that is, whether your love is unconditional—is revealed by who you're unwilling to run to. We all have a list of who we *would* run to. You'd probably start with the love of your life. I'm sure your children would be on the list. I think an even more helpful task would be to make another list: who are you unwilling to run to? Why? This is a concept that's very personal to me, because I've had people run to me when they had reason not to.

I need to tell you a story about me. Whether or not you read the rest of the book, it's important to me that you know it. I think it'll help with understanding what it looks like to run to someone. Now, I want to be the first one to admit I am constantly in need of God's grace and goodness! This book isn't a theory in my head; it's a real-life story I've lived. I'll prove it.

After graduating college, I moved to Manhattan, Kansas, to serve as a youth pastor. After about six months, I met Katy. Oh wow, I was hooked! I'd literally been praying God would one day bring an amazing woman into my life, and *boom*—He did. We fell in love quickly. I traded video games with my buddies for long walks in the park with Katy. We'd grab Sonic drinks late at night and talk in the outdoor kid's playground at the restaurant. We'd drink horrible coffee at Bob's 24-Hour Diner while we learned everything we could about each other. When I say horrible, I mean it was more like oil than coffee. But we didn't care, because Katy and I were falling in love. We went fast—so fast, we were undisciplined about our relationship. We didn't set up boundaries, so things got intimate very quickly.

I was a youth pastor in town. The teens I ministered to trusted me not only to teach them what the Bible said but also to model how to live it out. Their parents put that same kind of trust in me—trusting me not only to teach their children but also to show them how to live life. I also had a larger responsibility to the church I was serving at, to be a godly role model, an example others could follow. The stuff I taught the students about life, love, and dating ended up being something I wasn't living out. I was a hypocrite, and it was destroying me—and my relationship with Katy.

I will never forget a very specific December night when Katy and I both came to my house after visiting a store. Katy bought a pregnancy test. It wasn't long until we both learned our lives were about to change forever. We were going to be parents! Perhaps today's "normal" makes this seem like no big deal, but to us, it certainly wasn't how God intended us to start our lives together— secrecy, hypocrisy, and betrayal.

Immediately, I knew my tenure as a youth pastor had to be over. Even worse, I knew I had betrayed the trust of the teens, their parents, and the entire church! I submitted my resignation as youth pastor as soon as the office opened at the beginning of the week.

When you make choices like this, especially when you're in a church environment, the stories are often of people running away from you instead of to you. I didn't expect my situation to be any different. Katy and I knew we loved each other, and we decided to get married. But we figured the church saw us as public enemy number one, so we were gearing up to be publicly shamed. We'd heard stories about how Christians and churches were often mean and judgmental, so we expected the worst.

The week I resigned, a parent of one of the students I'd pastored called me. I knew what they were going to say. They were going to make sure I knew what a horrible example I'd been. They were going to verbally rip me to pieces. I expected it, and I knew I deserved it.

Instead, they asked if Katy and I would like to attend a Bible study they were hosting. The topic was marriage, and since they knew we would soon be getting married, they thought we might be interested.

We had no good excuse not to go. You know when you want to say no but your brain won't lock onto any intelligible excuse to offer? My thinking changed and grew even more full of shame—no more excuses, shame was telling me I deserved to get yelled at. Shame does that to you. It makes you feel like you deserve the worst punishment. So Katy and I took them up on their invitation.

We arrived at the house just on time. Both of us were terrified. Which one of them was going to yell at us first? How would they know we're sorry for betraying their trust?

I rang the doorbell, and the door opened right away. They were waiting and ready for us. As I started to awkwardly say hello, the couple who owned the home, Jim and Carol, stepped toward each of us and hugged us. I still cry when I remember this moment. Even as I type, tears are on my cheeks. This moment has yet to lose its meaning to me.

The words spoken first were from Jim and Carol, saying, "We love you both so much. We're so glad you're here." The other couples inside the house responded the same way. Hugs. Words of love and forgiveness. By the time we left, our relationships with them were already mending.

I got a call from Jim the following day, inviting Katy and me to attend church with them. Yes, the church where I *used to be* the youth pastor. Come on—that was off-limits to us, right? Visions of people staring at us with glaring, squinty eyes of judgment was what I thought would happen. Now, this church had never shown this kind of behavior, but shame told us it was inevitable. We figured we were no longer wanted there. We didn't necessarily think the people would hurt us, but we thought they might have some hurtful things to say about us.

I came up with excuses not to go for a couple of weeks. We'd be out of town visiting family, we were sick, I was considering a run for POTUS, etc. Even though we declined, the parents continued to invite us to church. They told us we could call them when we pulled into the parking lot so they could walk in with us and sit with us.

Katy and I finally agreed. I remember pulling into the parking lot and parking in the farthest spot from the church. As we sat in the car, I repeatedly asked Katy if she felt sick. Morning sickness—let's use this to our advantage! I was thinking of any excuse to turn around and drive home. But she felt fine. I had no choice but to make the call and let them know we were there.

When I opened up the car door, there was Jim. I had no idea how they found us so quickly. We had parked so far away. But they were there. And they walked into church with us, and they sat with us. Week after week, this was the routine until we began to walk in on our own. That is what running to someone looks like. That is love without conditions.

Consequences of Refusing to Run to Others

Not everyone is as fortunate as Katy and I were. There are plenty of people who do not know who Jesus is because people refuse to run to them.

Chances are, there are people who have hurt you or someone you care about, and you've refused to run to them because of what they've said or what they've done. Families get divided. Best friendships end all the time. Marriages implode. Co-workers take sides. We start loving by our conditions.

In this world today, there are people who don't know Jesus because other people disagree with their lifestyle or their political views. This is why I believe this book is needed. It's time the reputation of Jesus become the reputation of Christians! We should be known by our love for each other, not our judgment of each other. This is why I'm a pastor. I believe the church is God's appointed vehicle for this love. You can love a person and not endorse every decision they make. Parents, can I get an amen?

So, please allow me some room in your personal life to ask a question: Is there someone in your life you won't run to because of how they've affected you? Maybe even more directly: who are you refusing to love?

If you refuse to love someone because of their skin color, or where they come from, or how much money they have, or who they voted for, then it's time for us to work together on getting your heart healthier. God has so much more in store for your life! If I can have some pastoral permission right now, I would say your heart needs some help.

Jesus is willing to run to anyone and everyone. He dined with sinners and tax collectors (Mark 2:15). He spent time with both the poor and the rich and had conversations with people of all ages. Everyone matters to Jesus, and everyone should matter to us!

Jesus made this clear in John 13:34–35: "A new command I give you: Love one another. As I have loved you, so you must love one another. By this everyone will know that you are my disciples, if you love one another" (NIV).

Pay attention to the "as I have loved you." In other words, do you apply conditions to love and relationships Jesus didn't? Do you have "higher standards" than Jesus? Christianity isn't about the things you're not supposed to do or the types of people you're supposed to avoid. It's so much about love—unconditional love for God and for others. People will recognize you are a Christian based on how you love other people.

Oh, wait—I think this is where our pain can become an excuse. Let's make sure we understand love. Love does not require you to endorse the behavior of another person. Love does not require agreement on lifestyle or choices. Love is not limited by whether we agree with a person's worldview. Love communicates value. Running to someone isn't endorsing their choices; it's affirming they mean something to you. They carry the image of God and are worthy of His love, so you are willing to show love.

Our refusal to love certain people is dangerous. If there are people in your life whom you refuse to love, refuse to forgive, because of something they've done, then your standards are higher than those of Jesus Christ.

Jesus did not start the church as a place of specific political ideologies or cliques, or as an environment where only some are welcome. He started the church so every single person on this planet would have an opportunity to know Him. Many don't know who Jesus is because of what the church wasn't—but we can change this!

Choose to Care

So, what is the key to loving others with the right kind of love—unconditional love? *Love is conditional until you make it personal.* Jesus made love personal. Note that He said, "As I have loved you," in John 13. He made His love personal before He ever asked for us to do anything! It's crucial to know God's love if you're ever going to be able to love others well. Jesus said the model for love, the agenda for love, comes from how He loves us. Copy and paste, "the way He loves." He definitely didn't endorse everyone's lifestyle, but no one was too bad, radical, or different to get blacklisted from His lunch and dinner appointments. Making love personal like Jesus did enables you to love other people the way they should be loved, the way they need to be loved, the way that proves you have actually accepted Jesus' love.

But how do you make it personal if you just don't like the person? You must choose to care. Let me give you an example.

Say someone invites you to their kid's wrestling match. You show up, and then you find out that, out of the eight hours you're going to be there, the kid's wrestling match is only two minutes long.

It's the same thing when you go to a soccer game or a dance recital—two or three minutes of your kid's performance out of the hours you have to be there. Let me just say what every parent feels. Our joy isn't always found in the quality of the dancing or the number of goals our kids score. It's usually super-hot or super-cold at these games. Have you sat on aluminum bleachers for more than ten minutes? I'm confident hell has bleachers. I can't prove it, but I'm sure of it. So, why don't parents complain about all of this? It's because we're there for our kid. Why do we seem to adjust and figure out how to do it well? It's personal.

This is what choosing to care looks like! For the sake of your child, a niece or nephew, or a friend's child, you've spent hours waiting and watching to see them compete or perform. Chances are, the event wasn't the best concert any human has ever performed, and maybe they didn't remember all their lines, or possibly they missed a block on the football field—but that doesn't matter, because you chose to care.

It doesn't have to be a friend or family member you're choosing to care about. What about the waitress taking your order at the restaurant or the mechanic working on your car? Are you too busy going about your day, or can you choose to care and take a moment to ask how they are? If your son were your waiter, would you add a few extra dollars to the tip? You should. It's personal. If they're not your child, how about maintaining the perspective that they're *someone's* child. It's personal.

When it's personal, love becomes unconditional. But you have to care first.

Here's another example from a family at the church where I am a pastor. This is written in their own words:

> We have been blessed with six biological children and experienced the love and chaos and the highs and lows of raising five of them while losing one beautiful little girl.
>
> We realized there was a huge need in the community to care for children who, through no fault of their own, could not live in their family situation and often came from homes with very little stability. How can you eat at a table if you don't have a table—or food, for that matter—or "got to bed" when you sleep on the floor?
>
> We received a clear message from God regarding His calling to care for these children in desperate need of a safe home and unconditional love. In our twenty-seven months as foster parents, we have welcomed fifty-one children into our home, including three who have lived with us since our first day as foster parents.
>
> Our experience with foster care has been anything but easy, but it has been rewarding and improved the lives of many children in need. One of our biggest challenges has been to deal with behaviors related to trauma or substances that children have been exposed to prior to birth.
>
> We have been advocates for these children, to get them into counseling, to look for methods to improve their lives, and to help them heal through guidance, patience, and unconditional love. Prayer has carried us through

*the most difficult times, and God's blessings have been
the foundation for our home and carried the day.*

Caring for others, especially the most vulnerable, is a
mark of a true disciple of Jesus. This doesn't mean you
need to go out and sign up to become a foster family. But
you do need to start to care. Being aware of other people's
needs to be made personal. All too often, we become so
distracted by life, we only care about ourselves. But Jesus
gave us an example for how to love and care for others.

"The Offended"

We make everything personal, don't we? If someone
says something hurtful about us in real life or on social
media, we take it personally and we get offended.

We have become professionals at taking things personally and taking offense. It's hard to say anything without
offending someone. A publicized cultural value is tolerance, which involves putting up (graciously) with beliefs
or ways in conflict with our beliefs and ways. However,
tolerance isn't playing out, because it's completely mis-
understood. Tolerance has become understood as, "I'll
affirm your approach as long as you endorse mine."

Welcome to why so many people are offended. If you
see people based on what they do or don't do, you will get
offended easily. The unintended side-effect of this kind of
tolerance has become self-centered intolerance. In trying
to include, we are excluding. In trying to love, we're becoming less loving. And, the worst of it is, we are putting
all the focus on what we want and what we believe. This

creates problems. Yes, a society of getting offended happens, but it gets worse. In our pursuit of loving others, we've begun to make ourselves the focus. Now, the approach is, "You'd better endorse me, or you don't love me."

We're diminishing our ability to love anyone because we care most about what we want. Our spiritual hearts have become clogged with self-centeredness and a sense of self-righteous offense. How do we clear this blockage and clean out our spiritual hearts?

First, we must stop staying offended. You're going to get offended, and there's nothing wrong with that. I was called the "Pillsbury Dough Boy" as a junior in high school. I can picture that hallway and those lockers right now—I was hurt and offended. People will make fun of you and people you care about. They will say mean, hurtful things about you, and it's only natural for you to respond by being hurt.

But you don't have to set up a permanent residence in Hurtville! You don't have to change your name to "Victim." You can be hurt and acknowledge what happened was wrong, but then you can choose to keep moving forward in love. If it seems impossible to believe this, Jesus constantly gave us evidence that it's possible. In the book of John, it says, "He [Jesus] came to his own people, and even they rejected him" (John 1:11 NLT). Notice how it doesn't say how offended He was. Notice that Jesus eventually died for those people, too. Everyone gets offended, but everyone doesn't have to stay there.

Second, we must be willing to walk into "awkward." We must start walking forward by choosing not to be

trapped by the moments when we were hurt. This is awkward. As soon as you see that person at the store—
awkward. When an event, a date, or even a smell reminds
you of your past pain, awkwardly face it. You don't need
all the perfect words, or any words. Just stop avoiding the
hurt, and face it. If you want to have a healthy spiritual
heart, you need to quit giving awkward moments so much
authority.

This doesn't justify what the other person did to hurt
you. It simply means you are prioritizing the health of
your spiritual heart. Remember, above all else, we are to
guard our hearts (Proverbs 4:23 NIV).

Christians have a specific worldview: We believe in
the power of the resurrection. We believe Jesus was dead
and then resurrected. Your decision not to stay offended
could actually bring the power of resurrection to a relationship, or even better, to someone's soul. When was the
last time someone did something they shouldn't have
done and you were the first person to reach out to them?

Jesus told us the Parable of the Prodigal Son so that
you and I would have a heart like the Father's. We can
join the group of people who are constantly offended, but
we will die of spiritual heart failure. Our world needs
more people who are willing to give grace and mercy.

At multiple points in your life, someone has made love
personal for you. They got you a gift. They sent you an
encouraging text. They picked you up when you were
down. Maybe you screwed up and they chose not to cancel
you. That's when love is made personal and unconditional.

If you want to have a healthy spiritual heart, you know how to begin. Choose to care. Love unconditionally. And run to others even when—especially when—they seemingly don't deserve it. This is how God loves you, and this is how He calls you to love others.

WORKBOOK

Chapter One Questions

Question: How have you seen the condition of your heart impacting the relationships in your life? How do stress, hurt, and uncertainty affect how you interact with others?

_____

_____

_____

_____

_____

_____

_____

_____

_____

_____

_____

Question: Be honest and vulnerable with yourself and God: what is the current condition of your spiritual heart? On a scale of 0 to 10, with 10 meaning you simply can't get yourself any healthier, where would you rate the condition of your spiritual heart?

_____

_____

_____

_____

_____

_____

_____

_____

_____

_____

Question: Do you tend to run toward (in forgiveness) or away from (in bitterness) those whose actions have hurt you? Have you ever experienced a person or community running toward you even when you made a mistake? How did that affect you? What do you think is God's response to you when you make a mistake? How does (or should) that impact how you respond to others when they make mistakes?

_____

_____

_____

_____

_____

_____

_____

_____

_____

_____

_____

Action: *The health of your love—that is, whether your love is unconditional—is revealed by who you run to. The one you run to is who you love.* Let me encourage you to run to God. His arms are open wide. His heart is turned to you in love always. Whatever is weighing on you, whatever junk is causing a blockage in your spiritual heart, bring it to God. Bring it to the good Father who is ready to embrace you, cleanse you, and fill you with His love.

Make a list of the people you haven't wanted to run to. Begin to pray for each of those people every day. Your willingness (or unwillingness) reveals the condition of your heart.

Chapter One Notes

_____

_____

_____

_____

_____

_____

_____

_____

_____

_____

_____

_____

_____

_____

_____

_____

_____

_____

_____

_____

_____

_____

_____

CHAPTER TWO

Back It Up

Compared to our childhood, it's incredibly common for adults to give up on or shrink their dreams. Do you remember how big your imagination was as a kid? My kids have big dreams! My daughter's dreams have included owning a ranch and raising unicorns. Our family believes unicorns are real—and no, we can't prove it. One of our sons wants to impact the world via YouTube, and if given the chance, our oldest son would like to be a professional drummer who also designs high-end sports cars.

When I was a kid, I thought I was going to become a professional athlete. After missing the cut for the All-Star team my eighth-grade year, I began to realize I should devise some alternative plans.

As adults, we tend not to dream the way we did when we were kids, when all the possibilities of the future twinkled in our eyes. You could argue it's an age thing, that we become more realistic as we get older, but I disagree.

I believe God still gives people dreams, a vision for the future, no matter how old they are.

Why do we stop dreaming? Where does our eagerness go? Inadequacy is a huge reason. We're intimidated by the idea of what we hope to accomplish. Maybe someone told us we wouldn't be able to do it, or maybe we just don't believe we have what we think it takes. Either way, we give up before we've even tried.

You've heard of writer's block, right? Dreaming blocks are normal for us all. Inadequacy is a blocker. There's more, though: a lack of discipline can leave us with zero margin to even get a glimpse of the future. Without much effort, it can be easy to neglect or delay the work necessary to achieve our dreams.

You might want to be a doctor, for example, but you don't want to commit to years of medical school and hours upon hours of studying. Becoming a parent is a reason many give for why they laid their dreams down. What they're actually saying is, a lack of margin was their reason. Without margin, our dreams become "could've" and "should've" rather than reality. We don't stop wanting it; we just stop dreaming for it.

One more dream block deserves some attention. Sometimes we stop dreaming because we've been hurt. "Wow, David, you bring hurt up a lot." Yep. It's because I have yet to meet someone who isn't impacted by it. In fact, this might be the number one reason we stop dreaming. Our hearts have been wounded by people we care about, so much so that we no longer see the point.

As logical and practical as it may seem to stop dreaming, that doesn't change the profound truth the Bible has to say about dreaming and life in general. Remember this verse from Chapter One: "The thief comes only to steal and kill and destroy; I have come that they may have life, and have it to the full" (John 10:10 NIV).

Have you ever considered how this verse could apply to the dreams God gave you? Having a full life includes having dreams for how your future will look—dreams for a spouse, a family, your school, or meaningful work, and the impact you can have on the world. God made you, and He wants to accomplish great things through you!

When you have an unhealthy spiritual heart, your vision of the future, your understanding of life, becomes small and limited very quickly. It keeps you from dreaming. I'm not talking about sleep problems here. I'm talking about dreaming about the future—about what you can accomplish in life.

Proverbs 4:23 can continually steer us correctly. It keeps our minds honed in on the importance of guarding our hearts. I believe if we don't guard our hearts, we'll miss out on being a part of the great things God has in store for us. A feeling of inadequacy, a lack of discipline, and unresolved hurts are not part of the full life Jesus came to give us! They are symptoms revealing we need to give attention to the dreams God puts into our hearts—the attention He wants them to receive.

I'm a student of personality profiles. I've completed so many questionnaires that delve into my inner psyche. The reason I like them so much isn't that they give me a definition of "me." What I like is how they reveal what I've left unresolved. When you let the walls down, you can begin to utilize these profiles to understand how God wired you. You can combat the shame and regret we often allow to define us. Understanding what hurts have stuck and stayed around opens a door for healing those hurts. I have a craving I think you have, too: to have a heart all about what God wants. I want to love what I should love and deny what I should deny. And for my heart to be that way, it needs to be healthy.

More Than a Hug

I personally like to refer to the Parable of the Prodigal Son as Jesus' prescription for a clean spiritual heart.

When we left off, the son had decided to return home and beg his father to take him back as a servant. Any dreams the son had—of being part of his family again, of returning to his former life—seemed to have been squandered right along with his inheritance. I am sure he didn't feel like he deserved to dream.

And yet, in a display of unconditional love, his father ran to him, embraced him, and kissed him. But the story didn't end there.

You see, a healthy spiritual heart requires more than just a hug. It needs more than a declaration of love. All of us have had someone tell us something that later turned out to not be true. To be more specific, we've had someone indicate they cared about us, but their behavior didn't seem to demonstrate this professed love.

Sometimes people say something with good intentions, and then they don't back it up with their actions. All of us have done this, and all of us have been on the receiving end of this. Words or demonstrations of general affection can leave too much room for doubt. There needs to be something more.

Here's what the father did to back up his confession of love: "But the father said to his servants, 'Quick! Bring the best robe and put it on him. Put a ring on his finger and sandals on his feet. Bring the fattened calf and kill it. Let's have a feast and celebrate'" (Luke 15:22–23 NIV).

The best robe in the house would have belonged to the father. It would've had tassels hanging from the bottom that identified the family, almost like a family crest or a family seal.[5]

The ring was another item that would have identified the family. It would have been used to seal letters and show who had sent the letter. The son returned expecting to be treated like a servant—if he was lucky—but the father went above and beyond to make sure his son knew that he was still his son![6]

And killing the fattened calf for a celebratory feast? This wouldn't have been just any party. In Jewish culture, if you wanted to reconcile and restore a relationship, you would prepare a meal. The two parties who were at odds with each other would sit and talk, restoring the relationship over the meal.[7]

The father made sure his son—and everyone else—knew he had the family name and the family symbol, and that the relationship had been restored and the son was forgiven. This came at a cost. Literally.

What the father demonstrated here is core to understanding how love actually works. Love is not just a word; love is generous.

Love Is Not Enough

The eye-popping crazy part of this generosity is the timing Jesus laid out. The father gave and gave to his son before they even had a conversation. He hadn't yet asked the son if he knew squandering his inheritance was wrong, and the son had yet to confess any wrongdoing to his father. The father didn't know if the son had changed or if he was even going to take proper care of the robe and the ring.

We tend to think like that, don't we? We worry about enabling someone else's bad behavior or being taken advantage of. How many times have you hesitated to give to a homeless person because you were certain the money wouldn't be spent on the food their sign said they needed? Most of us are tempted to withhold a demonstration of love because of the possibility of being take advantage of.

But love alone cannot make a relationship work. Love by itself—as a feeling, as a desire, or even as words—is not enough. All of us believe this, but we don't always act like it.

Have you thought about this welcome-home reception from the son's point of view? What if his father had only offered him a hug and told him that he loved him? Based on experience and conversations with other people, I can tell you that the son would have lived in constant shame and insecurity. He would have wondered if he and his father were on good terms, second-guessing his standing. Even though his father said everything was fine, how could the son be sure he meant it without actions to back it up?

When someone tells you they love you, but then they don't support that statement with their actions, insecurity grows. The Parable of the Prodigal Son teaches us that love requires generosity.

We know all too well, love can be faked. Remember what it was like to have a crush in middle school? One day we would feel like we were in love with someone, but by the next day, those feelings had evaporated. We didn't have bad intentions. We weren't trying to be mean. We meant "love" in the moment—but then our feelings changed without warning.

Love without generosity—without giving, without sacrifice—makes for a shallow relationship. Imagine if I constantly told my wife, Katy, that I loved her, but then I didn't make time to talk with her and do things with her. What if "our" love was all about what she gave me? What if I did that to my kids? Sadly, this is where many relationships land. A love that was declared and intentional begins to suffer when the focus is all about the portion you're receiving.

So many of us have shallow relationships because we speak love and we intend love, but we don't *give* love. A healthy spiritual heart doesn't just say, "Everyone matters," and leave it at that. A healthy spiritual heart says, "And I'm going to do something to show them love."

God perfectly demonstrated the connection between love and giving, as expressed in John 3:16: "For God so loved the world that he gave his one and only Son, that whoever believes in him shall not perish but have eternal life" (NIV).

The key to this entire verse is the middle section: "...he gave his one and only Son." I think sometimes we get so focused on the gift, we forget God *gave*.

Yes, He gave us His one and only Son as the perfect sacrifice so our sins would be forgiven, which is amazing. But do not skip over how God loved you and me so much that He *gave* to us with generosity. He lost out so we didn't have to stay lost. Love gives.

God didn't just speak it or intend it. His love for us compelled Him to give to us! And because God gave to us, we know He means it when He says He loves us.

What has your love for God compelled you to give to Him? Some of you may be thinking, "Well, God doesn't need anything, so I don't need to give Him anything." Ah, now I know what kind of gift-giver you are. You're a socks, underwear, pots, and pans kind of a person. Bah humbug! Come on, you and I both know the only way to give gifts isn't merely based on what the person *needs*. Let's stop treating God this way.

We don't only give to our spouse or our children when they need something. We give them things they want and things they don't even ask for! I've given my children all kinds of ridiculous stuff they don't need, including toys they break in less than an hour. There is something thrilling about seeing the people you love light up with excitement!

Why should our relationship with God be any different? Shouldn't we want to excite God with our gifts to Him because we love Him? When you have gratitude for someone, when you love them and are thankful for them, you are compelled to give to them—whether they need what you're giving them or not.

It's fascinating how we can give anything and everything to multiple relationships, but when it comes to God, we can withhold that same level of investment because "He doesn't need anything." To me, this sounds like a lack of gratitude toward God!

Greed and Gratitude

Brene Brown has said: "...we're a nation hungry for more joy: Because we're starving from a lack of gratitude."[8] I absolutely agree with this. We've lost our ability to dream and some of us struggle to find any sort of joy in life. Maybe a reason is gratitude.

It's easy in this world to want more and more, to find the next thing you want and go after it. Gratitude starts to get difficult to hold onto.

A gratitude problem creates a greed problem. If you can't be grateful for what you have, you're always going to want more, and you're never going to be satisfied with it. Greed will enter your heart and make it unclean.

Greed is not an income problem, by the way. Rich people can be greedy, and so can poor people! It's a heart problem. It's an unwillingness to be generous with what you have.

We typically think of lust as worse or a more dangerous temptation, but in the New Testament, the Greek word *epithumeo* means "covet,"[9] and the Greek word *epithumia* means "lust."[10] There is only a slight difference in spelling between these two very dangerous words. Coveting and lust are from the same family. How we manage, give, and withhold resources can include a battle against coveting and lusting for more of it.

If you can't figure out how to give, how to be generous, then you're in danger of a dying spiritual heart. Consider the Dead Sea. The Dead Sea is the lowest body of water on the planet, and it is filled with so much salt that when the water laps against the rocks, the rocks look like they're covered in snow.[11]

I've visited the Dead Sea, and I can tell you that while it's beautiful to look at, it's really gross to get into. It's 34 percent salt.[12] It's a great one-time experience, but after you see what's left on your towel after drying off, you quickly decide one time was enough. Nothing can live in the Dead Sea, and there's a lesson to learn from this.

The Dead Sea earned its name because it doesn't flow out. This creates an environment where life cannot thrive.[13] Stagnant, standing, salty water can reflect the current state of our spiritual heart. If your love doesn't flow out with action, you'll get the same results as the Dead Sea: relationships won't survive your lack of pouring out. If gratefulness, joy, and happiness are a struggle for you, let's work together to pursue the abundant life Christ has for you (John 10:10)!

Greed is the leading cause of spiritual heart attacks. It clogs things up and stops the flow of your heart. It doesn't take long for greed to bring about spiritual heart failure and destroy your heart.

I have encountered many people who are angry, bitter, and completely broken in the worst sense of the word. As they shared their stories with me, it became clear this was because they stopped giving to God and others. I'm sure they wouldn't call it greed, but that's what it was. Greed took over!

Why do we get greedy?

Zero Is Comfortable

Think about what you do zero of. You and I both could make a list of things we're not interested in and plan to do "zero" of it. Now, apply this to generosity. Who do you give zero to? That's a long list and would take a while, so let's make this easy. On a scale of 0 to 100, how much of what you have do you give to God?

Nonprofits Source has assembled statistics about giving patterns in America.[14] According to the reports, Christians give, on average, 2.5% of their income to God. For comparison, during the Great Depression, that percentage was 3.3%. One could conclude a lack of money isn't our problem.

Also in the report, only 3–5% of Christians apply the "tithe" approach to giving to God. Tithing means 10%. It's a principle taught all throughout the Bible. It's not a way to earn God's salvation, but it's a principle that reveals the condition of your heart.

Here's something to consider with giving and God: Run away from zero. This is where many people are currently stuck—at zero. There are multiple reasons, but your heart needs you to run from zero.

A large portion of us give God "zero" simply because we don't manage our money well. It's not that we don't like God; we feel like we don't have enough to give Him.

When we feel like we don't have enough, we don't give anything. We postpone generosity until the day we finally feel like we have enough—and more often than not, that day never comes.

We're Our #1 Fan

We don't want to give our time or money to other people or to God because we want to keep our resources for ourselves. I know most of us don't put ourselves in this category, but it needs to be mentioned. We can easily get into a mode where we don't care enough about God or other people to give them a portion of what we have in our lives. It's easy to think only about ourselves and what we need.

We Forget History

In my opinion, this is the biggest reason greed takes root in our hearts. We forget God has supplied anything and everything we've ever had. I think the majority of people don't live generously simply because they have lost sight of how irrationally generous God has been toward them. As Jesus said, in Matthew 10:8, "Give as freely as you have received!" (NLT). Generosity is born out of our recognition of all we have received from God.

The Bible makes it clear, God is our provider. Consider James 1:17: "Every good and perfect gift is from above, coming down from the Father of the heavenly lights, who does not change like shifting shadows" (NIV).

When we forget this, we're in danger of becoming greedy. If we don't want greed to be a part of our lives and influence how we live, we need to make a point of remembering what God has done.

> *Be careful that you do not forget the LORD your God, failing to observe his commands, his laws and his decrees that I am giving you this day. Otherwise, when you eat and are satisfied, when you build fine houses and settle down, and when your herds and flocks grow large and your silver and gold increase and all you have is multiplied, then your heart will become proud and you will forget the LORD your God, who brought you out of Egypt, out of the land of slavery.*
> **—Deuteronomy 8:11–14** *(NIV)*

This is a powerful lesson to learn. If you deny or choose to forget that God provides all you have, your heart is in danger. Many of us have started to think we are our own providers, which is simply not true.

Remembering what God has done for us takes practice. Get into the habit of thanking Him for providing you with a job and an income whenever you receive your paycheck. While you're doing your grocery shopping, you can thank Him for giving you food to eat. When you're helping someone—whether it's a family member, a stranger, or someone in your church—thank God for providing you with an opportunity to give to others. After all, everything you have is ultimately from God!

Generosity Starts Here and Now

So, what do we do now? Begin where you are, with what you have. God will never ask you for something you don't have, so don't wait to be generous. The early Christian church didn't wait to be generous. They gave from what they had, to God and to others.

> Now I want you to know, dear brothers and sisters, what God in his kindness has done through the churches in Macedonia. They are being tested by many troubles, and they are very poor. But they are also filled with abundant joy, which has overflowed in rich generosity. For I can testify that they gave not only what they could afford, but far more. And they did it of their own free will.
> **—2 Corinthians 8:1–3** *(NLT)*

God never intended our giving to be focused on the amount. It's all about the intention and the sacrifice—potentially inconveniencing ourselves and needing to change our lifestyles so God and others can benefit from our generosity.

Let me share an example with you. Just before Hurricane Harvey hit Houston, Texas, in 2017, El Bolillo Bakery sold out of bread and baked goods as residents stocked up ahead of the storm.[15] Most of the employees were able to get home safely to their families, except for four of the bakers, who ended up trapped at the bakery. You can imagine how happy they were to be stuck there, especially during a violent hurricane.

When we find ourselves in a bad situation, all we want is to get out of it. But these bakers decided to make something of their situation—literally.

They knew Hurricane Harvey was going to do some serious damage to their city and people were going to be in need when the storm lifted. And one of the things people were going to need was bread.

These bakers baked their way through four thousand pounds of flour. They replenished everything that had been purchased and then some. Every rack in that bakery was filled.

They could've just made enough bread to get themselves through the storm. No one would've blamed them for that! Or they could have hunkered down and done nothing. No one would've blamed them for that, either!

Some of you may be thinking, "Well, of course they're going to replenish what they sold. When the hurricane stops, they'll be in a position to make a lot of money!" But that's not what the bakers did. They packaged up all the bread, and as soon as the storm let up, they went to as many shelters as possible and gave away everything they had baked!

A person who is willing to give resources is a person who is able to give hope. Willingness is a big deal! Get away from zero.

Are You Willing to Give?

We all run into people who are unwilling. Unwilling to forgive, to help, to give, to support, to be involved, to have a conversation.

But then there's that whole other crew, the people who *are* willing. The friend you call to help you move. The family members who will always be by your side. The church who is willing to walk with anyone. Or like the father from the story of the prodigal son, who was willing to display irrational generosity to a son who felt unworthy of love.

When Katy and I were first married, our income was barely enough. In fact, our income wasn't enough. Katy was a college student at Kansas State University while working very part-time at the KSU Alumni Association. Mix that income with my unsuccessful daily search for a job and you come up with a need for government and family assistance. The government covered milk and cheese and many medical needs for Katy and our young son, Hayden. However, we still had cost-of-living bills. The longer I looked for a job, the smaller our savings account became.

One day, my grandma called to ask if she could help us. It wasn't a secret to my family that my job search in a small town was making everything tight. Every bit of my pride wanted to say, "No, Grandma, we've got everything covered." She pressed. That's how my grandma rolls— she wants the honest truth. She asked what our mortgage payment was each month, and at the time, it was around $900. I told her the truth, and we finished the conversation on the phone. I knew she was sending money, and I had hope we would make it through another month.

Within a few days, we received a card from my grandma. Inside of it, she told us how much she loved us and was rooting for us. Inside the card was a check for the exact amount of our mortgage.

Let me pause the story for an important detail. When Katy and I were dating and just married, we'd had multiple money conversations. We discussed how we would spend and save money. We even determined we would be a generous family; it would be a value to guide our lives. A goal of ours has long been to increase the percentage of money we give away every year, if possible. Young couples have big aspirations—wink, wink. No, we've not been successful every year, but we try. We were firm that no less than ten percent of any money landing in our hands would go to our church home. This principle is taught all throughout the Bible, and we were going to own it! We simply couldn't imagine not giving back to God.

With that detail about how Katy and I had pre-planned to treat money, now I can bring up our quandary. We had nearly zeroed out our savings, and two major expenses stared us in the face: we needed to buy groceries, and we needed to pay our mortgage. But my grandma sent a check to cover our exact mortgage! Problem solved, right?

No, because before that check arrived—well, remember the whole thing about generosity to God that Katy and I had committed to? It's easy to write down values before pressure challenges those values. We'd agreed we would return to God ten percent of anything that ever crossed our hands. Birthday money, anniversary money, paychecks— all money.

I remember staring at the check my grandma sent, praising God for His provision. We still had a choice: give to God, pay the mortgage, or get groceries. We could only choose two of the three options.

We immediately wrote a check for ten percent of the check my grandma sent. We wrote it to our church and readied it for when we'd go to church on Sunday. God was going to get His portion first. Then we paid our mortgage company. Groceries were entirely up to God.

I wonder if "that's foolish" just crossed your mind? Or maybe, "God would never ask someone to go without food," was a thought? I am not one to say God always sends money to those who give Him money. I'm not one to ever suggest God makes a person rich when they give to Him. Frankly, that's heresy. What I do believe is, God always provides if you trust Him with what He gives you.

After the check was written and bills paid, we'd emotionally understood the month was going to have some days we literally wouldn't eat.

I came home the next day after spending the entire morning job hunting. Sometime around 1 p.m., someone knocked on our door. I went to answer it, assuming someone was selling something. Recently I'd let a vacuum salesman come and give his pitch to me because he offered to clean our couch and gives us a two-liter bottle of Dr. Pepper. Come on in, my friend!

The gentlemen at the door wasn't a salesman. It was a sweaty guy covered in dirt, and "stank" doesn't even describe what was filling my nose. He said, "Hey, you don't know me. I've been living a few houses down, and I'm moving today. I can't take all the food in my fridge and freezer with me, and I don't want to throw it away. Would you want all my food?" Was he kidding me? I said, *"Yes!"*

The guy brought over frozen roasts, hamburgers, noodles, and canned food. He even brought over an opened container of soy milk. I'd never tried that before, let alone with it already opened, but who cares when you have no food, right? (By the way, I quickly learned I am not a fan of soy milk. Don't suggest almond milk to me, either. How do they squeeze milk out of almonds, anyway?)

My point is, you and I can debate how much a Christian should give to God. Personally, I can't imagine our family keeping more than ninety percent of what God gives us. That's seems crazy-generous of Him, to set up a precedent of only ten percent. Personally, I will always avoid zero at all costs. You and I can have a friendly conversation about interpreting what the Bible says on generosity to God. Is it ten percent, or is it thirty-three-ish percent? We can debate the percentages, but what's not up for debate is the miracles I've experienced in my life.

On multiple occasions, God has provided exactly what we needed, when we needed it. I believe it's directly connected to giving to God. You simply can't outgive Him. As a family, we're determined to honor God with generosity to Him and to others, and this single decision is the area of our lives where we have seen the most miracles.

As a pastor, I've had many conversations with people about money and God. It's got to be the topic most commonly on people's "how to offend me" radar. Could it be that our sensitivity to the topic might be a sign of how important sacrifice and finances should be taken?

I used to evaluate how a church spent "my" tithes and offerings. Were they managing my hard-earned money efficiently and effectively? I don't do that anymore. Now I don't care if they go cash it at the bank and burn it in a fire pit. Why? Because I don't give to God and place intentions on it. I'm not buying a "good church." I'm giving to God. In fact, in the early days (read the Old Testament), people would bring their generous gifts to the church and literally watch the guy burn the gifts in front of them. Generosity isn't a purchase or transaction. It's submission and acknowledgement that God is good and hope is real.

To be able to give hope, you must be willing to give. To be able to give love, you have to be willing to give. To give anything good—realize the simplicity of our mandate—be willing to give. A clean spiritual heart requires us giving to God and others. He can multiply what we give to Him, and He can do amazing things with it. He can do miracles with it, like with the boy who gave Jesus five loaves and two fish. Jesus multiplied these and fed five-thousand people (John 6:1–14)!

With a clean spiritual heart, a heart not clogged by greed, irrational generosity flows freely. I believe that this perspective of gratitude and generosity is what fills us with the ability to dream again. When we realize all we have been given, we can't help but dream big, God-given dreams that will bless God, yourself, and others. Run, as fast as you can, away from zero.

Chapter Two Questions

Question: Do you have dreams? Do you have visions for your future? In what ways do you need to allow God to reignite your passion for the life He's called you to? What is one dream you have for the next ten years, and what's one thing you hope to accomplish twenty years from now?

_____

_____

_____

_____

_____

_____

_____

_____

_____

_____

Question: What has your love for God compelled you to give to Him? Have you found yourself believing God doesn't need to receive from you because He doesn't "need" anything? What ways can you give generously to God moving forward?

_____

_____

_____

_____

_____

_____

_____

_____

_____

_____

Question: Is your life categorized by ingratitude and an inability to find joy in the present? What do you think is the root of your lack of joy, feeling like you don't have enough, and the subsequent greed? What do you think is the key for moving to a place of gratitude and irrational generosity? Is money an area where you allow faith to grow? Are you willing to return a portion of your money to God each time you're paid?

_____

_____

_____

_____

_____

_____

_____

_____

_____

_____

_____

_____

Action: Let a desire to give generously be born out of the knowledge of (and gratitude for) God's generosity toward you. Spend some time in God's presence. Allow Him to show you all the ways He has blessed you, cared for you, and enriched your life. If it helps you make it more tangible, start a list to recognize all the things you are thankful to God for. Ask Him to show you how you can be irrationally generous today, this week, this month? What can you do for someone else that requires you to sacrifice—to give something up or change something in your life in order to bless them?

On a scale of zero percent to one hundred percent, how much do you give to God? What percent are you willing to start at with your next paycheck? What percent will you move to in three months? Six months? One year from now? And who will you ask to keep you accountable for this?

Chapter Two Notes

_____

_____

_____

_____

_____

_____

_____

_____

_____

_____

_____

_____

_____

_____

_____

_____

_____

_____

_____

_____

_____

_____

CHAPTER THREE

Unwavering Mission

In 1781, General Cornwallis and the redcoat army entered Yorktown.[16] This wasn't their target destination. Bill Bennett knows how to tell the story of history so well. Here's how he details it:

> The patriots to the south had wreaked havoc on his redcoat army, and he was hoping to rendezvous with the British Navy on Chesapeake Bay.

> American and French troops, however, anticipating Cornwallis's plan, pounded them with cannon fire, while the French fleet cut off escape by sea. The British found themselves trapped.

> Thomas Nelson, then governor of Virginia and a signer of the Declaration of Independence, was fighting with the patriots firing the cannons in Yorktown. Gathering the men, he pointed to a beautiful brick home. "That is my home," he explained. "It is the best one in town. And, because of that, Lord Cornwallis has almost certainly set up the British headquarters inside."

And he told the American artillerymen to open fire on his own house. They did. As the story goes, the very first cannonball shot at Mr. Nelson's house sailed right through the large dining room window and landed on the table where several British officers were eating.

What an example of a life on a mission. Unfortunately, our current day-in, day-out lives can feel absent of a mission worth living (or dying) for. A lack of a sense of mission is what has many of us discontent. When you list your greatest accomplishment for the day as putting your laundry away or updating your phone, it's easy to quickly wonder if life has anything else to offer.

I wonder what your calendar looks like. I use an app to remind me of where I need to be and when I need to be there. I love how flexible it is—actually, I love how it buzzes me when I need to go to a meeting.

My wife uses papyrus, an ox bone shaped into a pen, and ink made from petroleum and oil as she documents her schedule inside a leather-bound binder colored with the perfect shade of pink. I'm kidding. She's going to be mad at how I describe her beautifully assembled three-ring planner, which is artfully detailed with stickers and color-coded designations. It works well for her. She likes it. I will stop teasing her. The bottom line is, her process definitely helps our family manage our schedule.

We have four kids and a dog. Scheduling monthly haircuts can be an overwhelming project. It's easy to feel like life is a little too full. It's not uncommon to lose control of our calendars and desperately crave a break. Whether you use a smart watch, a desktop computer, or a binder, we all know a packed-full schedule can happen fast.

Jesus offers a full life, but this doesn't equate to a full daily schedule. He said He came so we "may have life, and have it to the full" (John 10:10 NIV). When something is full, it is satisfying and extraordinary. Full isn't always about quantity. Jesus came to give us a satisfying and extraordinary life, which doesn't automatically mean an overcrowded schedule. "Satisfying and full" also doesn't mean "perfect and pain-free."

Instead of having nothing, Jesus wants us to have everything we need. Instead of a bland and pointless existence, He came to give us purpose. This does not mean our lives will be absent of problems and quandaries, but it does mean we do not have to submit to life's demands, priorities, and expectations. Jesus didn't come so we may have life, and have it jam-packed with the meaningless and mundane.

The full life is God's desire. Sounds pretty amazing, doesn't it? But it also contradicts the story of many of our lives. There doesn't seem to be much about our lives that is satisfying or extraordinary.

Would a life with positive impact be a full life you would want? I know we want to raise our kids in the right way. We want to be the spouse we promised to be on our wedding day. We want to be the business owner, the employee, the friend, the person who truly contributes, adds, and makes our circles better. That certainly sounds like a satisfying life to me!

But to have this full life Jesus came to give us, we need to have clean spiritual hearts ready to engage life as God intended. There is a mission required to make this happen.

Unwavering Mission

Let's discover the final ingredient in Jesus' prescription for a clean spiritual heart revealed in the Parable of the Prodigal Son. Thus far, we know this prescription includes love, which is then connected to generosity. In this chapter, we'll discuss the third and final element: a mission.

Where we left off, the father had welcomed the son back into the family by dressing him in the best robe, putting the family ring on his finger, and preparing a feast to reconcile with his son and celebrate his return. But not everyone in the family agreed with what the father did.

> *The older brother became angry and refused to go in. So his father went out and pleaded with him. But he answered his father, "Look! All these years I've been slaving for you and never disobeyed your orders. Yet you never gave me even a young goat so I could celebrate with my friends. But when this son of yours who has squandered your property with prostitutes comes home, you kill the fattened calf for him!"*
>
> *—Luke 15:28–30 (NIV)*

The older brother's reaction may seem reasonable. It's practical. And it's crucial we understand the significance of his refusal to go into the party. Why did Jesus continue the story after the movie-ending, tear jerking reunion of the father and son? Why didn't He pan out as we mentally picture a beautiful party and a restored relationship?

In Jewish culture, reconciliation would take place over a shared meal. By not going into the party, the older brother was communicating he didn't want to forgive his younger brother. It wasn't fair to him. He refused to accept his father's response to his younger brother. He did not want to restore that relationship.

Here's how the father responded:

> "My son," the father said, "you are always with me, and everything I have is yours. But we had to celebrate and be glad, because this brother of yours was dead and is alive again; he was lost and is found."
> —*Luke 15:31–32* (NIV)

Our world needs more than love and generosity. It also needs people willing to love and be generous in specific ways. In other words, rather than random, we need more people loving and giving with a mission.

The father refused to forget he was the father. He refused to waver in the role he committed to. His mission was to be a good dad. He knew a good dad would not give up on his kid or let circumstances, choices, or even his own pain and disappointment strip him of his mission.

Many people do not experience this with their own parents. You might have already been thinking as much, before I brought it up. Maybe your dad wasn't a good dad, or your mom wasn't a good mom. Many people have experienced a romantic relationship where the other person wavered and didn't remember what they said they would be to you.

One way or another, we've all been in situations where someone faltered, wavering in what they said they would do or what they were supposed to do, and abandoned their mission.

I played Little League baseball as a kid, and I was in love with the game. What makes leagues like these even better is if you land a great coach. For my seventh-grade year, I had *that* coach. Coach Henry knew the game, and he cared about us as young men. I played catcher for our team, and I had a really good season.

I have fond memories of that year, one being when I was at the plate with a three and two count at the bottom of the last inning. (Translation: I was the batter, and I had a chance to win the game for our team if I got a hit.) The pitcher was one of the best in the league—Robert Ashbrooke. He was a friend, but on the field, we were mortal enemies. He pitched a fast ball right down the middle, and all I remember is making solid contact with the ball (he says I closed my eyes and swung). I ran as fast as I could while my teammate scored from third base. We won the game. I hit the winning base hit! What an amazing end to an amazing season! Ah, the glory days.

When the next season came around, my last as a Little Leaguer, I was so excited for another season with my favorite coach, Coach Henry. However, I had a problem come up. My family had plans to be out of the country during the time of the tryouts. My parents talked to the league, and they agreed to let my name remain in the "draft." Coach Henry planned to make sure I was on his team.

When we got back from overseas, we contacted Coach Henry to find out when practice started. He had news I didn't expect: another coach picked me before he had a turn to pick. I would be playing for a different team. The coach who picked me up was the coach of the team I'd hit the game-winning hit against. I would eventually learn he picked me specifically so he could bench me on his team for the entire season.

This new baseball season was the opposite of the previous season. I was brokenhearted. My coach had to play me two innings per game, per league rules, so he usually put me in during the middle of the game, in the outfield (a position I'd never played). He would pull me out with two innings left in the game. One time, he submitted the substitution incorrectly, so the ump said I had to stay in for the rest of the game. I ended up hitting a game-winning homerun and earning the coveted "game ball." To say the least, my coach wasn't happy about it.

I'm telling you this because I don't think my coach started coaching for the purpose of taking out grudges on young boys like me. I think he loved the game like I loved the game, but winning and revenge became his mission. I'm going to give him the benefit of the doubt and say he did what many of us have done: he unintentionally wavered from his mission.

By definition, *waver* means to become unsteady or unreliable,[17] to falter.[18] Maybe you're making a mental list right now of all the people in your life who have been unreliable, who faltered. Before we start throwing stones, let me make something clear: we are all susceptible to wavering.

Every one of us has been tempted to waver—to just walk away. Pressure, disappointment, or maybe fatigue ushered you to the point of just being "done." Perhaps a role you committed to got stale. Can we all be willing to admit we struggle to stay committed to our responsibilities every day, especially when pressures rise?

Wavering, although common, can create some unintended damage and a lack of fulfillment. I've had many conversations with people whose spouses have wavered in their faithfulness. The result was a spouse's broken heart.

I've talked with teenagers whose parents weren't there when they needed. I know friends who thought they had loyal friends, only to discover they didn't. The result is always the same: hurt and heartbreak.

So many of the extra-difficult times' and most painful hurts arise when someone wavered from what they committed to. They didn't fulfill appropriate expectations. This is why the Parable of the Prodigal Son is so crucial. It's not just about love and generosity. It's about not forgetting who you are and what you said you'd do. It teaches us not to allow pressures, tension, culture, or other people to deter you from what you should be doing. That is the heart of possessing a mission.

The Importance of Convictions

An unwavering heart requires healthy convictions. Maybe you're in a dating relationship and you want to set boundaries for physical intimacy, but you find yourself wavering from your morals. It's amazing how alone time with your significant other can become an immediate challenge to what you believe is best, versus what you want in the moment.

If you've ever struggled with an addiction and you plan to stay on the right path, you're well aware of the wavering you're tempted to do when you spend time with the wrong people again and again.

If you want a life guarded by a mission, attention must be given to your convictions. They need to be defined—written down, put on your mirrors. You need friends reminding you. Convictions are so important; they have the power to keep you from wavering.

In Luke 15:32, the father said, "But we had to celebrate and be glad" (NIV). Think about when you've used the words "I have to." That's you making a statement about your convictions. It implies you have chosen not to have a choice about what you are going to do. In fact, you are intentionally and adamantly choosing a specific direction.

That's the power of a conviction. When you build them into your life, they can become dependable and actually lessen some temptations. Convictions are an intense internal sense of, *"In order to be the person I promised to be, to fill the role I am supposed to fill, I absolutely have to do this!"*

We usually make decisions one of two ways: according to our convictions or according to our preferences. Consider how you decide what to eat. According to your doctor, what you eat should be based on your convictions. You should choose foods that will keep your body healthy and nourished. However, eating based purely on our preferences is an easy rut to slide into. My preference is BBQ ribs, donuts, movie popcorn with lots of butter, and sweet tea. However, my doctor says if I go with my preferences,

I'll get a less-than-preferred outcome. You see the lesson coming, don't you?

The Supreme Court has weighed in on this matter. Not on what foods we should eat, but on the difference between a preference and a conviction. According to the Supreme Court, "A preference is a strong belief, but a belief that you will change under the right circumstances. A conviction is a belief that you will not change."[19] Too many of us change the important things in our lives based on our feelings in any given situation.

Our oldest son has always been drawn to any kind of vehicle with an engine. We knew, early on, he would want a driver's license and car as soon as the law allowed. We make a deal with our kids: we'll match whatever they have saved for the purchase of a vehicle. (Yes, if one of our kids decides he wants to be the best money-saver ever, I'm in trouble.) Anyway, Hayden has been saving and saving. His problem is, he wants other things as well. If Apple releases a new phone, Hayden is aware. If the Jordan brand releases a retro shoe, Hayden is aware. Okay, full disclosure, I'm aware too.

Throughout the years of saving, our son has had moments when Airpods or a pair of Jordans became more important than the future purchase of a car. I am impressed, however, at the way he continued to save—and it's paid off. He's the proud owner of a quality, used Honda Civic. Rarely do any of us ever accomplish a mission perfectly. A completed mission, not a perfectly executed mission, is always the goal.

When you wake up and before you put your feet on the ground, start considering your first big decision of the day: will you be mission-focused today? What is your "but I have to"? We need more people with an unwavering mission in life, like the father in the story!

Do you know God has convictions? We can identify them in Scripture by paying attention to what He is most passionate about, what He dwells on, and what situations cause Him to intervene. One of His convictions is expressed in John 3:16: "For God so loved the world that he gave his one and only Son, that whoever believes in him shall not perish but have eternal life" (NIV).

God's love for us is one of His foremost convictions. He was willing to sacrifice in order to rescue and restore us! He wants anyone and everyone to know who He is. This is stated even more directly in Luke 19:10: "'For the Son of Man came to seek and to save the lost'" (NIV).

Embracing God's Convictions

Our convictions make up the rhythm of our spiritual heartbeat, and it is the same with God. If we want our hearts to beat in rhythm with His, we need to embrace His convictions.

You're allowed to have your own preferences and convictions regarding things like what you eat, but there are three important convictions you need to have in common with God—convictions so powerful that nothing will ever change them.

The first is that Jesus Christ is the hope of the world. That should be true in our hearts no matter what we do, who we spend time with, who we marry, who we raise in our house, where we work, or what we do with our lives.

It should be our mission for our spouse, our children, our co-workers—everyone we encounter—to know Jesus Christ is the hope of the world. A relationship with Jesus is the most important relationship we can have in this life! He is the source of hope, and He will never fail us. God so badly wanted this, He showed up here on earth to make it so.

The second conviction is that the local church is the best investment in the world. Our time, talent, and treasure should be invested in the local church.

Let's consider Jesus' life for a moment here. Jesus did not start a hospital. Hospitals are good and necessary, but He did not spend His time starting a hospital. Neither did He start a business, or even a charitable organization. Again, both are important. However, Jesus did start something: the church!

Jesus said to Simon Peter, "And I tell you that you are Peter, and on this rock I will build my church, and the gates of Hades will not overcome it" (Matthew 16:18 NIV). During His limited time on earth, Jesus invested in the people who would become His church. We would be wise to do the same! As we've already discussed, Jesus is the hope of the world. The local church—not the building itself, but the Christians who gather there—is the delivery system of this hope.

The third and final conviction is that the best way to show people Jesus is to serve them. Jesus spent much of His time on earth serving others. He healed the sick. He washed His disciples' feet. He didn't scream at people who disagreed with Him or make passive-aggressive posts on social media. He served people. We do too much screaming and not enough serving!

Jesus made it clear how important it is to Him that we serve others, in Matthew 25:40: "The King will reply, 'Truly I tell you, whatever you did for one of the least of these brothers and sisters of mine, you did for me'" (NIV).

Service begins inside your home and expands outside to your local community, and then to the global community. Remember, when you serve someone, you are not just serving them. You are serving God!

No Turning Back

What does conviction look like? One of my favorite examples is a group of people from the turn of the twentieth century known as the one-way missionaries.[20]

Instead of heading out to the mission field with ordinary luggage, they packed their belongings into a coffin. They purchased a one-way ticket to their destination because their intention was to show Jesus to the people there until they died. Those people would then place their body in the coffin and bury them. The one-way missionary had no intention of ever returning home. Talk about conviction!

One of these missionaries was A. W. Milne.[21] He sensed God calling him to a tribe of headhunters in the New Hebrides, known today as Vanuatu. This was a people group that had martyred every missionary who came to them. When Milne arrived, however, the tribe let him live.

He lived with them for thirty-five years, showing each of them Jesus before dying of natural causes. The tribe buried him in his coffin, and on his headstone, they wrote, "When he came there was no light. When he left there was no darkness."

I want to be worthy of having those words on my headstone. I want to go to a place and be a part of something where I bring light. What if you became a one-way missionary? You don't have to go to an isolated island. It can be a state of mind, with a goal to be a deliverer of hope.

I am convicted Jesus Christ is the hope of the world and the local church is the delivery system of that hope, and I am going to serve people whether I like them or not.

Evaluate Your Convictions

Have your preferences distracted you from God's convictions? It's easy for this to happen to any of us. Think about your current preferences—how you treat people, how you live, what you do with your time and money. The convictions we hold will always show up in how we live our lives.

It's not about our ideals; it's about what we actually do with our lives and whether we live by our preferences or by God's convictions. That will reveal to us if we live in unwavering mission.

We must refuse to ignore the lost and the least, those who feel abandoned, isolated, and forgotten. As we live fueled by God's convictions, we will experience the full life Jesus promised. When we live according to our unwavering mission—fulfilling the roles we have committed to and doing what we have promised to do—we shine light into the darkness.

WORKBOOK

Chapter Three Questions

Question: What does being faithful look like to you? Describe a moment from your own life when you saw faithfulness represented.

_____

_____

_____

_____

_____

_____

_____

_____

_____

_____

_____

Question: Is your life characterized by the fullness and abundance Jesus promised? Why or why not? Are you prone to wavering in your commitments?

_____

_____

_____

_____

_____

_____

_____

_____

_____

_____

Question: Have you ever experienced someone who failed you or let you down? What did you feel as a result of that experience? What does that reveal to you about the value of possessing an unwavering mission?

_____

_____

_____

_____

_____

_____

_____

_____

_____

_____

_____

Question: What are your most important convictions in life? Read the list of convictions in the section "Embracing God's Convictions." Do you share these convictions?

_____

_____

_____

_____

_____

_____

_____

_____

_____

_____

_____

Action: Ask God to show you what your unwavering mission in life should be. Take some time in prayer, in the Word, and in God's presence and write out the convictions you have, and the convictions God wants you to have. Use these to write a "mission statement" to keep at the forefront of your mind as you endeavor to shine God's light into a world of darkness.

Without worrying (for the moment, at least) about restrictions of probability or ability, write out a list of possible "one-way missionary" missions you could undertake. Take your ideas to God in prayer, and then draft a specific mission statement for one of the ideas.

Chapter Three Notes

_____

_____

_____

_____

_____

_____

_____

_____

_____

_____

_____

_____

_____

_____

_____

_____

_____

_____

_____

_____

_____

CHAPTER FOUR

Keep Showing Up

In theory, we could stop this journey together since you now have three core values worth building your life on. A marriage could easily adopt "Love, Give, Go" as its mission. A church could easily use it as their mantra to guide themselves to be a church resembling Jesus. Parents, bosses —I even know principals who have used it to guide their school. However, most of us want more specifics. I would suggest most of us need more specifics.

I struggled in school. What class did I struggle with? Pretty much all of them. My parents never had a bumper sticker that said, "My child is an honor roll student." I'm not against rolls—I just prefer the cinnamon kind. (Sorry. I debated on adding the "dad joke," but it *rolled* so naturally into this part of the book. I'll try to *rise* above these inclinations.)

So, school. I didn't do well. Can you guess why? My main complaint, all the way through was, "But, how does this philosophy turn into practical application?" I started college on academic probation, but I did graduate. Barely. Eventually, I applied to do my master's degree. They accepted me with open arms and the status of academic probation.

However, something clicked differently for me with my master's, compared to my previous education. Now we were pushed to apply everything, immediately. I thrived! I got straight A's (except for a class that involved going to Israel, because somehow I got a B+ for a class that only required I show up).

I wholeheartedly believe knowing history, philosophy, and principles is absolutely crucial. Principles are so important to me, I started the book with them as the foundation: love, give, go! But in addition to values, we need to figure out *how* we can live them out practically, day after day. Values require motion or they aren't really values, right?

Our first way to add a spark to values so they also become behavior: *show up, and keep showing up.* You can make this even more specific, like showing up to weekly worship with your church. I know, stereotypical thing for a pastor to say. Ever wonder why pastors say that? I'll tell you the secret agenda—you ready?

We gather so we can meet God in a special way and He can meet us. The early church, as detailed in the book of Acts, says they devoted themselves to gathering together to worship. It can be a struggle to go to church because we feel it's difficult to find one we like, one we feel comfortable in, or one we agree with completely. Be careful with this approach. Chances are, you don't share the same preferences with every person in your life. You may differ in regard to the foods you like, the music you listen to, or the football team you cheer for.

Church preferences are not necessarily bad, but they should come with a warning label. If we choose to lock down some of our preferences and refuse to budge from them, we can lose people in our lives as a result. This is especially true when it comes to political preferences. I continue to be told story after story of conservatives who are cancelling their liberal friends, and liberals who are cancelling their conservative friends. When relationships can no longer exist because of differing approaches to governance, I believe we have stepped away from the model Jesus showed us.

How much do you know about Simon the Zealot, one of Jesus' disciples?[22] That's not his last name—that's his approach to politics. He was a part of the Jewish nationalistic party who longed for independence for the Jewish nation. An offshoot of the Zealots were the Sicarii, also known as daggerman. They were a group who tried to physically fight against the Romans.

Simon the Zealot was a part of the Twelve, the close disciples of Jesus Christ. That's important to know, because a man named Matthew was also a disciple and a Jew, except Matthew worked for the Roman government, collecting taxes for them *from* Jews.[23] These two men figured out a way to coexist with different political preferences, and then they helped change the world together.

I'll be the first to say, one of the potential lures of preferences is how they can so quickly and easily bind us together. They can help create a friend group where you go to the same movies, or maybe your kids play on the same team. I'm a part of a small group that, yes, likes Jesus, but we meet once a month for the purpose of smoking meat. That's one hundred percent preference. That's one hundred percent of the reason my vegetarian friends won't attend that small group.

But a danger exists, too: preferences can separate us and cause rifts between us. They can isolate us. We feel and experience this daily.

If we don't pay attention to the warning label on our preferences, we could find ourselves at odds with people we should never be at odds with, and specifically, disconnected from groups of people who could actually be encouraging and challenging us to walk with Jesus.

I believe the divisiveness going on in our world has leaked into the church. Many Christians may be wondering what even unites us. We all have a long list of preferences, all the way down to which Bible translation we prefer to read. But as different as we all are, God calls us to come together in unity. The lesson here: don't allow your preferences to be your excuse for not showing up. That negatively impacts you and the church.

The Importance of Unity

Unity within the church was so important to Jesus, He asked God for it:

I am praying not only for these disciples but also for all who will ever believe in me through their message. I pray that they will all be one, just as you and I are one—as you

*are in me, Father, and I am in you. And may they be in us
so that the world will believe you sent me.*
—John 17:20–21 (NLT)

When Jesus takes time to pray and it's documented in Scripture, we should pay attention! Most of us are familiar with the Lord's Prayer, yet we tend to overlook this prayer.

Our oneness as a church has everything to do with people knowing who Jesus is. This prayer makes it clear that even though our world is full of anger and disunity, the church doesn't have to be—because of Jesus! Whatever our preferences may be, Jesus is what we share in common.

This concept is further emphasized in 1 Corinthians 1:30: "God has united you with Christ Jesus. For our benefit God made him to be wisdom itself. Christ made us right with God; he made us pure and holy, and he freed us from sin" (NLT).

Jesus is what brings us together, no matter what our past says about us or where we come from, and no matter what our race or gender is. And yet, many people believe that most Christians are counterfeit Christians because of the lack of unity and love they see among us. Jesus called us to be united. We need to be people who sincerely care about other people, with an agenda of worshiping God.

The Solution Starts with "Me"

Healthy begins at the individual level. Our natural tendency is to criticize the bigger group, the larger organization. In other words, we usually first find fault with the company we work for, the league president of our kid's team, or the elected officials in our city before we address our own contributions and the efforts we've invested. We tend to justify our own behavior, thinking our need to change isn't as important as their need to change. We acknowledge their elevated responsibility but use it as an excuse to negate our own. Frankly, it's easier to have expectations of the bigger group than to hold ourselves as equally accountable.

The easy response to a bad experience is to treat the experience as your reason "why." I have friends who tell me they struggle with church, and their "why" is an experience—an unmet expectation. As a fourth-generation pastor, I assure you that I have many stories of negative experiences in church across the nation. However, Jesus' church will always have people. This means Jesus' church will always be imperfect. If you are part of a collective group and you want that group to get better, then you as an individual need to get better, rather than avoiding the group all together. Showing up is a mature response, so needed in today's world.

If you are part of a family and you want your family to get better, then it begins with you being better. If you want your workplace to be better, the best way for you to contribute to that is by starting with yourself.

The same is true in marriages and friendships. If one person gets better, the health and potential of the whole relationship increases.

Many of our problems seem overwhelming until we realize that we can play a role in fixing them. This is about personal responsibility, how to own our responsibilities and not project them onto a pastor, a church, or even God.

So, how do we do this? How do we get better? It starts with a commitment to show up.

God Is More Than Our Rescuer

God didn't create the world and then abandon it to function on its own. He has been actively involved with humanity throughout history! He desires a personal relationship with each and every one of us.

Unfortunately, many of us have a very one-sided approach to that relationship. We tend to operate from a posture that God loves us so much, He'll simply interrupt us when we need to be interrupted. He'll stop us when we need to be stopped. He'll make us go when we need to go. We put the entire responsibility for that relationship on God.

My wife, Katy, and I have experienced something very similar in our home. All four of our children had an early approach to life, especially in their first year. If anything was needed or wanted, we were the ones who fulfilled those needs and wants. It's Parenting 101.

For example, before our youngest, Bo, was able to crawl, if he wanted or needed anything, we had to bring it to him. If he wanted a toy lying a foot away from him, we had to get it for him and bring it to him.

I miss those days, because once he learned how to crawl, we moved into non-stop rescue mode. Our role became saving Bo from himself! Despite our best efforts at childproofing, he was brilliant in figuring out how to access everything—drawers, cabinets, you name it.

There is a season of parenting when you spend a great deal of brain cells, and burn through some adrenaline, consistently swooping in to grab a kid as they're on the brink of destroying themselves in a full-body tumble down the stairs or in a skydiving attempt from a couch. That phase of parenting should be made into a warning label or a book.

Eventually, our kids grew out of this. We've parented enough to know they will not always need us to swoop in and grab them at the last second (the keyword being "always"). One goal as a parent is for your kids to no longer rely on you as their primary means of survival and head-injury protection.

My concern for many Christians is when they decide to follow Jesus but maintain the same approach with God that our children gave us when they were young. Sometimes people stay in toddler mode with God, and the only time they experience Him is when He interrupts them in the midst of their mess, their falling-down moments.

Many of us have incredible stories about different occasions when God stepped into our lives and rescued us. That is by no means a bad thing! But if we only experience God at rock-bottom moments, when He steps into our emergency, we are missing out on so much more that God offers us in our relationship with Him!

I want you to have a rich relationship with God. But just as my children have to mature to experience a richer relationship with me, you will have to mature to experience a richer relationship with God.

Showing Up Is Key

Henry Blackaby is one of my favorite writers, and he has written a great deal on the topic of experiencing God. The approach he advocates isn't always what we find naturally easy.

Blackaby sums up his approach like this: "'What is God's will for my life?' is not the best question to ask. The better inquiry is, 'What is God's will?'... Once I know God's will, then my life gains its proper perspective, and I can adjust my life to Him and to His purposes."[24]

The turning point is when we start asking how we can join God in what He's already doing. That's how it looks to mature in your relationship with God, to get outside of religion and grow beyond God having to do anything and everything in your life.

Here's another gem from Blackaby: "He never speaks to us simply to increase our Biblical knowledge. Our Lord has far more significant things to reveal to us than that. When God shows us what He's doing, He invites us to join Him in His activity."[25]

Last, but certainly not least, my absolute favorite quote out of all of Blackaby's writings: "...watch to see where God is working. If God shows you where He is working, immediately join Him!"[26]

The best way to experience God is to show up and keep showing up. For many of us, we showed up once, or even several times, but then there came a moment when we stopped showing up. You've likely witnessed how the demise of a marriage begins when someone stops showing up mentally and emotionally, or how the demise of a job begins when an employee stops showing up. A drift occurs.

Drift means to "wander aimlessly."[27] Most of us would say we aren't "aimless," but our lack of showing up consistently can be a better diagnostic tool about how much drift exists in our lives. A vulnerable time with a friend might produce an honest assessment of how intentional you are. Every one of us has blind spots, and in my experience, every one of us is at least slightly less intentional than we think—myself included. It's proof of our need for others in our life, to help encourage and challenge us.

Many of us have not intentionally pursued worshiping with others as an absolute necessity. Am I only talking about showing up at church? No, attending church isn't the only way to experience God, but it's definitely a central part of it. The key principle here is about showing up and continuing to show up. Show up to meet God when you read your Bible, when you work, when you worship by yourself, and when you worship with your church. The distance between us and God is often felt, close or far away, based on whether or not we're showing up.

Lukewarm Christianity

Scripture makes it clear that showing up for God is incredibly important. One of Jesus' harshest warnings on this matter is recorded in Revelation 3:15–16: "'I know all the things you do, that you are neither hot nor cold. I wish that you were one or the other! But since you are like lukewarm water, neither hot nor cold, I will spit you out of my mouth!'" (NLT). Jesus directed these words toward the church of Laodicea, which He described as having a "lukewarm" attitude. The Laodiceans weren't cold or hot in relation to God, just lukewarm.

Let me give you a little context here. In the city of Laodicea, water was brought into the city via six miles of aqueduct.[28] [29] The problem was, after a six-mile journey, the water was not particularly fresh when it arrived. It wasn't hot or cold. It was on the fence—disgustingly lukewarm!

Some scholars have said the city had a distinctly unpleasant odor because of this water.[30] [31] The water wasn't usable in the condition it arrived in, either. In fact, if you drank it as is, it could cause you to vomit!

Jesus used an example from the everyday life of the Laodiceans to warn them about their spiritual condition. Even today, we understand lukewarm water is not the most appealing or usable water. No one wants a glass of lukewarm water after a workout! Hot water has value because it can cleanse, purify, and even soothe. Cold water has value because it can refresh. But lukewarm water has very little appeal.

This is one of the harshest truths Jesus ever put in front of us. It is not only for the church in Laodicea, either. Lukewarm Christianity is detestable to Jesus—He spits it out of His mouth!

If you like factual studies about people's behaviors, consider this. There was research done, including Christians, over the course of ten years.[32] The researchers asked participants lots of questions and closely observed their behaviors. They discovered that people who claimed to be Christians interpreted the commitment in varying ways.

Some who claimed to follow the way of Jesus didn't show any signs of that commitment. Others who claimed to be Christians seemed to be incredibly passionate and "on fire for God."

The study found that these Christians who were on fire for God—who got off the fence of indecision—had certain characteristics. First, their relationship with Jesus brought them deep joy and satisfaction. Second, Jesus spoke to them in a way that was relevant to their lives. And lastly, worship was a lifestyle for them, not just an event.

Notice, the Christians who didn't live in the way of Jesus didn't express joy and satisfaction in their relationship with Jesus. They didn't have much to say about hearing from Jesus in a relevant way. Most strikingly, worship wasn't a "lifestyle" for them. It appears that showing up to meet with God has a ton to do with actually having a thriving relationship with Him.

I'm not trying to guilt you or shame you into doing more. My hope is that you'll recognize how unsatisfying life on the fence can be. Joy. Happiness, relevance, worship—they're not found on the fence.

Most of us are completely unsatisfied with anything counterfeit. Counterfeit money. Fake knock-offs. It's time we saw lukewarm Christianity as counterfeit Christianity. Being on the fence is counterfeit Christianity. That approach toward God is nauseating to Him. Jesus made it clear that the church at Laodicea was a dead church. Their lukewarm faith was hypocritical, and their church was full of counterfeit Christians.

On-the-fence Christians are some of the most danger-ous people on earth! They claim a lot, but they don't live it. They might sometimes be physically present, but they're not mentally, emotionally, or spiritually present. They don't show up.

If you are envisioning a better church for our nation and our world, it begins with you becoming a better "you." And that means getting of the fence and being an authentic Christian!

Do you have any of the top three characteristics of a Christian who has gotten off the fence? If you don't, it's okay—you're not the only one. This is an opportunity to grow.

Hold Tightly to God

The Bible says in Hebrews 10:23, "Let us hold tightly without wavering to the hope we affirm, for God can be trusted to keep his promise" (NLT). If you don't want to be a lukewarm Christian—if you want to be the best version of yourself—you need to hold tightly to God. By holding tightly to God, you keep other things from holding tightly to you.

Many of us could make a list of the things we're hold-ing onto tightly. Perhaps you've decided to go on a diet or start a new exercise routine so you can have a healthier physical heart, and you're holding tightly to these new habits.

A couple of years ago, exercise wasn't a part of my life. I would have told you at the time, exercise is vital for a healthy lifestyle. I would have told I should be exercising.

I would have agreed with all the experts: if you want to live the life you should, then exercise!

My agreement with the need didn't mean I was actually exercising. It was a thought. Internally, I felt bad about this. I felt like a hypocrite. I knew there was a better way to do life, and I knew I'd need help getting this to be a part of my life. So I joined a gym and got a buddy to be my personal trainer.

I held tightly to that new exercise program. During a sermon, I even told my church about it, in hopes that doing so would keep me accountable and encourage me to stick with it. And I did stick with it! I didn't cancel. I didn't quit. I was pretty proud of myself.

But then I had to go out of town. I had no choice but to cancel my gym session. My personal trainer gave me a set of exercises I could do at my hotel to make up for the missed session.

Of course, I didn't end up doing those exercises. I didn't hold tightly to this interim exercise routine and instead held tightly to other things—like enjoying myself, resting, and trying some new restaurants.

I came back to town and resumed my workout program, but then there came a day when I woke up and just didn't feel like working out. Hard to imagine, right? So I canceled my gym session that day. After that, it became easier and easier to cancel.

We've all been there. When we stop holding tightly to something—when we stop putting effort into it and avoid taking personal responsibility—other things creep in. In my case, I was clinging to potato chips, doughnuts, and other unhealthy foods that would drive my doctor to despair.

Likewise, we need to let go of the things weighing us down and hold tightly to God. When COVID-19 stepped into all of our lives, I found it extremely difficult to turn off my brain from questions of how to lead my family and our church. It was nearly all-consuming. People quickly began taking sides. There were theories, conspiracy-theories, and facts. For me personally, how to lead our church and love people well felt like an impossible calculus equation to be solved. Whatever answer I arrived at, people would both affirm and revolt. So, I did something I've preached over and over.

I worshiped until my worry submitted. I literally played worship song after worship song throughout the house. I didn't ask my wife or kids if they cared—it was just going to happen. I did this day after day, and my worry took a back seat to my God. Don't assume I had all of the answers—no way. But I had peace, which is always better than the answers to my questions.

We cannot put the responsibility for our relationship completely on Him. This is more than religion! In a relationship, people hold tightly to each other. Let Jesus' plea to the Laodicean church motivate you to hold tightly to Him. Jesus longs for you to be more than indifferent to Him. He wants someone who will show up fully in the relationship.

Show Up, and Keep Showing Up

That's how we grow. If we continue to show up and keep growing, we will increase the potential for the groups we're a part of to improve.

There have been many days when I only showed up to work out because my personal trainer was already there—because I knew he made room in his schedule for me and I would be inconveniencing him if I cancelled, so I showed up even when I didn't want to.

If we keep showing up, we will motivate one another. Hebrews 10:24–25 says, "Let us think of ways to motivate one another to acts of love and good works. And let us not neglect our meeting together, as some people do, but encourage one another, especially now that the day of his return is drawing near" (NLT).

We need to think of ways to motivate each other so we do not become counterfeit Christians. And we need to encourage each other in light of Christ's imminent return so that when He comes back, He does not find us on the fence as lukewarm, hypocritical Christians. When He comes back, let Him find us off the fence!

A Better "Me"

If we want to be better collectively, you and I need to start having conversations about ourselves as individuals. You and I need to stop saying, "That's about them," or, "They need to change this or improve that." We need to ask ourselves, "What am I doing?" and, "What can I do better?"

If you are struggling in life right now—if you feel like you've already thrown your life away and don't see the point in showing up for your own sake—show up for someone else. If you feel like you are in the depths of darkness and you don't have the energy to experience God and hold tightly to Him, simply support the person in front of you.

You may not have any consideration for yourself right now, but perhaps you will consider another person and how much they need you—like how I show up for the sake of my personal trainer even when I don't feel like showing up for myself. My personal trainer couldn't force me to show up. I have a responsibility in all of this.

Things begin to break down in this world when Christians don't take responsibility. I encourage you to take responsibility for your relationship with God and show up—for your sake, for His sake, and for the sake of others.

God loves you whether you show up or not. But He desires for you to play an active role in what He is doing, and you can only accomplish this by showing up.

Let's be the difference! May we each be a better "me" by showing up consistently—at church, in our workplace, in our marriages, in our families—so that collectively we can be better.

WORKBOOK

Chapter Four Questions

Question: Do you value unity with the people in your life? Share a moment when you or someone else contributed to maintaining unity in your home, workplace, or school. Are you more focused on trying to change others or on changing yourself? Have you ever tried to change, and succeeded in changing, something in your life? Explain.

_____

_____

_____

_____

_____

_____

_____

_____

Question: Do you only experience God as a rescuer when you find yourself in need of help? What does this reveal about your relationship with God? How can you grow to experience God consistently in every facet of your life? Where are you weak at "showing up"?

_____

_____

_____

_____

_____

_____

_____

_____

_____

_____

Question: Do you have any of the top three characteristics of fully devoted Christians? Which ones do you have? Which ones are least reflective of you? What areas do you need the most growth in?

_____

_____

_____

_____

_____

_____

_____

_____

_____

_____

Action: Showing up for your relationship with God is the best way to grow. Make involving God in your life and spending time with Him an intentional priority. Perhaps start by making an appointment with Him every day and keeping it. Start small and work your way up. The more time you spend with God, the more you will want to spend time with Him. Keep showing up!

Chapter Four Notes

CHAPTER FIVE

Share Hope

Multiple times in my life, leaders with far more experience let me have access into their lives. My dad and mom have done this my entire life—allowed me honest access to how to be a good husband, parent, and pastor. I've had multiple pastors let me enter their world to learn around them and from them. Still, to this day, I am regularly at someone's "table" who has already experienced what I'm experiencing. These moments of learning are a crucial moment of hope for me. I always walk away feeling more confident and ready to take on the season God has me in. My soul is full of hope, and I'm ready to lead.

No one wants to be a lukewarm Christian who lives on the fence. That really doesn't need to be said, but not everyone realizes they need help learning how to receive and give hope. This is essential to being a follower of Jesus. Not only do we need to show up for God and for others, but we also need to share hope.

One of my favorite stories in the Bible about sharing hope can be found in 2 Samuel. It starts in 2 Samuel 4:4 (NLT):

> *(Saul's son Jonathan had a son named Mephibosheth, who was crippled as a child. He was five years old when the report came from Jezreel that Saul and Jonathan had been killed in battle. When the child's nurse heard the news, she picked him up and fled. But as she hurried away, she dropped him, and he became crippled.)*

Mephibosheth was the grandson of King Saul, who was the king of Israel until God replaced him with David due to Saul's disobedience (1 Samuel 15:28). Mephibosheth may not be a name you're familiar with, but let me tell you, this story is absolutely relevant to your life.

I will give you some historical context beyond what the Bible says. When a king died in battle, that meant he lost the battle and the entire royal family was in jeopardy.[33][34] Oftentimes, the royal family would be wiped out as a result, and the only way to avoid this fate was to make a run for it.

According to the history books, when Mephibosheth's nurse picked him up to flee and dropped him in her panic, both his legs were probably broken.[35][36][37] They were then likely set improperly, which meant he would have grown up crippled, unable to do things most of us take for granted. This part of the story is a big deal.

As time passed, Mephibosheth faded from public memory. He went from being royalty to having no meaningful reputation.

David Remembers His Covenant

Then, this happened: "One day David asked, 'Is anyone in Saul's family still alive—anyone to whom I can show kindness for Jonathan's sake?'" (2 Samuel 9:1 NLT).

At this point, David had ascended to the throne and was king over Israel instead of Saul. To be clear, he was not a member of Saul's family. David started a new dynasty. But Jonathan was David's best friend. They made a covenant with each other that they would take care of each other for the rest of their lives (1 Samuel 20). As part of this covenant, Jonathan requested that if anything happened to him, David would take care of his family.

Some people may have been skeptical as to why David was asking if anyone from his best friend's family was alive. They probably thought David would want to kill any survivors from Saul's dynasty to keep them from revolting against him. But this was a sincere question on David's part because he wanted to honor his covenant with Jonathan.

David asked this of Saul's former servant Ziba, who told him, "Yes, one of Jonathan's sons is still alive. He is crippled in both feet" (2 Samuel 9:3 NLT). That isn't the most politically correct way to describe someone, but Ziba said it for a reason. He wanted to make sure David knew Mephibosheth was not a threat to him or his throne. In that culture, people with handicaps or disabilities were ostracized and considered useless.[38][39]

David wanted more information, however, so he asked for Mephibosheth's location. Ziba told him he was in Lodebar, at the home of Makir son of Ammiel (2 Samuel 9:4). This may seem like a throwaway statement, but in the context of the culture, Ziba was again emphasizing that Mephibosheth was not a threat. He revealed Mephibosheth's life situation, essentially telling David that he was not able to provide for himself. Mephibosheth couldn't grow his own crops or tend to his own animals. He didn't own his own home, and lived with another family. He was completely dependent on other people!

Mephibosheth was likely born in the palace. Now he was living in obscurity and relying on other people to take care of him. He had been so completely forgotten that the king had to ask if anyone from Jonathan's family was still alive.

There are life circumstances in which it would be easy to lose hope and give up on your dreams. If we're honest, we've all identified with Mephibosheth at some point in our lives! We've all had moments when we stopped dreaming because it seemed pointless—times when we felt insignificant, overlooked, and forgotten.

But everything was about to change for Mephibosheth!

From Riches to Rags to Riches

When David discovered where Mephibosheth was, he sent for him and had him brought before him (2 Samuel 9:5–6).

Mephibosheth probably thought his life was over. Remember, in that culture, it was David's right to kill any survivors who remained from the previous royal family. It's no wonder David told him, "Don't be afraid!" (2 Samuel 9:7 NLT).

David then continued, "I intend to show kindness to you because of my promise to your father, Jonathan. I will give you all the property that once belonged to your grandfather Saul, and you will eat here with me at the king's table!" (2 Samuel 9:7 NLT).

This was amazing, incredible news for Mephibosheth. His response shows us just how hopeless he had been feeling. "Mephibosheth bowed respectfully and exclaimed, 'Who is your servant, that you should show such kindness to a dead dog like me?'" (2 Samuel 9:8 NLT). His emotional state was such that he saw himself as a dead dog—worthless and completely without hope.

Again, I think many of us have been there. Whether it's due to decisions we personally made or circumstances that are beyond our control, we've felt like we're not nearly as worthwhile as we hoped we would be. We've all had moments where we longed for hope!

Being a good king, David didn't only announce the news about the change in Mephibosheth's situation to Mephibosheth. He also made sure other people knew, and issued instructions so this change would actually come to pass:

Then the king summoned Saul's servant Ziba and said, "I have given your master's grandson everything that belonged to Saul and his family. You and your sons and servants are to farm the land for him to produce food for your master's household. But Mephibosheth, your master's grandson, will eat here at my table." (Ziba had fifteen sons and twenty servants.)

—2 Samuel 9:9–10 *(NLT)*

Not only would Mephibosheth have his own property, his own household, and a seat at the king's table. He would have hope in his life, too, and other people would help him have that hope.

This is how things ended up for Mephibosheth: "And Mephibosheth, who was crippled in both feet, lived in Jerusalem and ate regularly at the king's table" (2 Samuel 9:13 NLT).

There would've been a variety of people eating at the king's table—members of the royal family, high-ranking officials, military leaders. These were people with power and responsibility, who made important decisions and put their lives on the line for the sake of the kingdom.[40][41]

Mephibosheth had no power or authority. Yet the king gave him a place at his table! David had no desire to take from Mephibosheth; he only wanted to give to him abundantly.

Share Hope

The story of Mephibosheth teaches us that hope isn't only something we should want to receive; it's equally as important to share it. Don't you want to be the kind of person who can give hope to the hopeless?

As Christians, we received hope when we acknowledged we couldn't save ourselves and accepted Jesus'

offer of salvation. We believe hope is available to everyone, regardless of their past or where they come from. We
should share that hope as much as possible.

But here's the problem. Many Christians stop at receiving their hope, instead of sharing it! They have claimed
and welcomed hope into their lives, but they don't realize
sharing it is equally as important.

Your Story, Their Hope

If you want to be Christian who is off the fence of
counterfeit Christianity, sharing hope needs to be a priority for you. This doesn't mean you stand on the corner
wearing a sandwich board and yelling at people. There are
all kinds of ways you can share hope with others.

Hope is often best delivered through your story. Each
one of us has a story. As Christians, our stories have moments when we have decided to turn to Christ and
moments when God has come through for us. You have a
story of you and God encountering each other. You need
to share that! First Peter 3:15–16 (NLT) phrases it this way:

> *Instead, you must worship Christ as Lord of your life. And
> if someone asks about your hope as a believer, always be
> ready to explain it. But do this in a gentle and respectful
> way. Keep your conscience clear. Then if people speak
> against you, they will be ashamed when they see what a
> good life you live because you belong to Christ.*

We need to be able to tell people how and why we have
hope. Your story is the best place to start! We don't

necessarily have to open up the Bible and walk people through God's plan of salvation. We can start by telling people how we encountered God and received His hope.

In Romans 1:12, Paul said, "When we get together, I want to encourage you in your faith, but I also want to be encouraged by yours" (NLT). The power of your story of challenge, of victory, of trusting God, could encourage someone else in their story.

Don't worry about how ugly your story might be or how tame it might seem or whether it has enough tragedy. Tragedy isn't what makes your story good. Your story is good because it has God in it.

And remember, you and I are not the main characters in our stories. God is. It's all about Him and what He has done for us and in us.

Chances are, there's someone in your life who needs to hear your story because their story needs to encounter God. Your story could be the spark that gives them hope! But your story can only deliver hope if you tell it. This is the main reason I share many of my own personal stories with you. I'm not sure it helps you to know the weird, wild moments, often of poor judgment, in my life. I do know what helps me, though: borrowing some hope from another person. That usually happens via their personal story, but I'm going to share a story with you that I was told.

In 1999, a governing board determined the church I pastor (I wasn't pastoring at the time) needed to close its doors. It was decided the church would cease to exist. At the time, bills were a struggle to pay and pastors were cycling in and out like the wind. I'll spare you the horror stories I've been told, but apparently, there are people to-day who don't go to church anymore because of how badly the church used to treat people. Maybe you or a friend have had a similar experience—a bad experience when "church people" mistreated you. From what I can gather, the church was essentially dead. There wasn't any sign of spiritual life.

Before the official vote was taken, a man spoke up and suggested the group pray about whether or not to make such a final decision. That decision to pause led to an eventual decision not to lose the church. The good news: the people began to function a little heathier. The bad news: the change was really only behavior, not heart.

When I was hired as the pastor of the church nearly nine years later, I unknowingly walked into a battle. People had strong opinions about what a pastor should and shouldn't be like. Trivial things were made major issues. Any change I made was greeted with intense conversations. After three months on the job, I went home after church on a Sunday. I walked into our home, saw my wife standing there in the kitchen, and immediately started sobbing. I told her I was quitting. I didn't want to lead a church more concerned about the placement of flowers on a table than about people who don't know Jesus. Katy looked at me and simply said, "No, you're not quitting. We're not moving yet."

I have to confess I lean toward the selfish side of the attitude barometer. Meaning, when Katy didn't show any sympathy, I was immediately mad at her. I know better than to start an argument, so I went to our back bedroom and decided to start an argument with God. I led with some opening statements: "God, do You understand how much I've done for You? Why are You letting my life be so difficult? I moved my family to South Dakota to pastor a church, and You're not really helping much!" (That's the edited version appropriate for a book written by a pastor. Wink, wink.) I spent some time telling God all I'd done for Him.

Then, there was ... silence. I was tired. I waited for an audible response, frankly because I felt like I deserved it. "Come on, God. Just once. Talk to me out loud."

Then, a thought crossed my mind:

"David, what are you willing to do for Me?"

"Um... God, if that thought was from You, did You not hear my ranting I've been doing? I told you what I'm willing to do. I'm happy to repeat it if necessary."

Silence.

Then another thought crossed my mind, and three words were added from the last one: "David, what are you willing to do for me *as a pastor*?"

I knew the right answer: "Whatever you want, God." So that's what I told Him. I decided in that moment, I wouldn't try to be a good politician-pastor, trying to accommodate everyone's wishes. I would risk my job by listening to God and doing whatever He asked. And from the very next week, and still to this day, people began showing up to church, trying to figure out how God was relevant to their lives. Over and over, people would tell me, "I'm not sure why I'm here, but I just felt like I should go to this church today."

Broken marriages have been restored. Addicts have been freed from addiction. Lost people have decided to follow Jesus and live for Him. Kids, teenagers, and adults have found the power and peace of a relationship with God. Lives have been changed. It's absolutely incredible what God has done in and through this church. What once was a dead church is now alive. Oh, and it just so happens to have a pastor who has his own story of how he was spiritually dead and is now alive.

That, my friends, is the significance of sharing your story. Fountain Springs Church was spiritually dead. I told you a story already of how I used to be the same way. Now, because of God, I once was dead and now am alive. Fountain Springs Church was once dead and is now alive. That's two stories.

What's your story? I would guess God has completed some portions and He's still working on other portions. That's at least how it's playing out with our church and my own life. It's time you started sharing what God has done in your life. You have at least one story someone else needs to hear.

Share Hope by Sharing an Invitation

Hope can also be delivered through an invitation. Sometimes the people we care about have problems we cannot fix—and maybe we shouldn't try to fix them! But we're overwhelmed with sadness for them. We want to help them in any way we can.

The best thing we can do for them is to invite them into our lives. We can invite them out for dinner or coffee and offer them a listening ear. We may not know how to give them hope, but we can invite them to church, a place where God often shows up and delivers hope.

Doing this requires bravery. I think many Christians have stopped inviting people to church or into moments where we can talk about hope because we're afraid of how people will respond to us. We've lost some of our courage!

This is not a new problem. In 2 Timothy 1:8, Paul said, "So never be ashamed to tell others about our Lord. And don't be ashamed of me, either, even though I'm in prison for him. With the strength God gives you, be ready to suffer with me for the sake of the Good News" (NLT).

If you're finding your faith is lukewarm, if you're on the fence, your issue might be that you're ashamed to tell people about Jesus Christ and your faith in Him.

There is an absence of hope in this world because Christians are not realizing we need to live in courage. Courage isn't something we need once or twice a year. It has to be a regular feature of our lives!

People might not respond the way you hope they will respond. They might reject Jesus, and they might reject you. But there has always been risk associated with delivering hope.

Saving Lives and Bringing Hope

Back in the late 1700s and early 1800s, there was an organization called the United States Life-Saving Service. It was run entirely by volunteers. Think of it as a volunteer fire department, but along the coast.[42][43]

Stations were built on the shore to store small boats and other rescue equipment and were manned by volunteers. Shipwrecks were common then, as this was before there were lighthouses all up and down the coast. And wherever a ship wrecked, that was where its crew and passengers died—unless they somehow managed to swim to shore.

Volunteers would watch from their stations to locate any ships in distress. When they found one, the volunteer would send up a flare, get into their boat, and go out to rescue the people on the wrecked ship.[44]

These volunteers risked their very lives to bring hope to people they didn't even know! They didn't question whether the people they rescued were at fault for their predicament. As soon as they saw a ship in distress, off they went.

One of the United States Life-Saving Service regulations was, "You have to go out, but you don't have to come back."[45] Volunteers signed up with the knowledge they might die while attempting to rescue people. They knew every time they went out, there was a chance they might not return.

Here's another one of their regulations: "The statement of the keeper that he did not try to use the boat because the sea or surf was too heavy will not be accepted unless attempts to launch it were actually made and failed."

You would think you shouldn't say things like this to volunteers, but they did. And it worked! The modern-day Coast Guard has even incorporated some of the regulations of the United States Life-Saving Service into their own.

The United States Life-Saving Service still exists, but they don't save lives anymore. According to their new mission statement, they are "dedicated to preserving our national life-saving treasures."[46] They have an annual meeting, and they still get together to share meals and visit old life-saving stations. But they are no longer rescuing people.[47]

Take Courage and Take a Risk

The story of the United States Life-Saving Service shares some similarities with the church. Most churches were started by Christians in areas where they believed with everything in them that people needed to know hope, needed to know who Jesus is.

But there are many churches that have completely abandoned that original mission! It's not about sharing hope and sharing Jesus anymore. It's all about trying to preserve traditions, preferences, or simply the way things used to be. And of course, who's bringing what for coffee hour!

Most Christians want healthy churches. Obvious, right? Churches are made up of people. The best approach to a healthy church is for Christians to individually address their personal lives. It starts with you being a better "me." Our churches get healthier as soon as the Christians who belong to them actually begin to go out and share hope with others.

Your bravery is someone else's access to hope. Your story has the power to give hope to others if you will be brave enough to share it. Your courageous invitation for others to join you in life and at church could give them access to the hope they have been praying for.

As we share hope, we will risk our relationships, our popularity, our acceptance—a lot of things that could make our lives uncomfortable or awkward. But consider the risks if we don't share hope! People to whom God is ready to deliver hope will not receive it because we were afraid.

Don't do that. Don't be that. Tell your story more, and extend more invitations to others. Watch how God works through your willingness to take risks so that others may receive hope—and Jesus!

Chapter Five Questions

Question: Is there a moment when someone made you feel special? Have you ever felt like you didn't matter to anyone? Like you were insignificant, overlooked, and forgotten, and like your life didn't have a purpose? How did that feeling affect your ability to have hopes and dreams for your future? How did you cope with that feeling, and what was the outcome?

_____

_____

_____

_____

_____

_____

_____

_____

_____

_____

_____

Question: Make a list of ways you can bring hope to people.

_____

_____

_____

_____

_____

_____

_____

_____

_____

_____

_____

Question: What fears or insecurities keep you from reaching out to others—inviting them into your life, inviting them to church, or sharing hope with them? How do those fears hold up in light of what God's Word promises to those who faithfully serve Him?

_____

_____

_____

_____

_____

_____

_____

_____

_____

_____

_____

Action: Take some time to write out your story. Involve God in this process and allow Him to show you all the times and ways He was there for you throughout your life. Let this process fill you with hope, and ask God to show you how and when you can share this story of hope with others.

Chapter Five Notes

_____

_____

_____

_____

_____

_____

_____

_____

_____

_____

_____

_____

_____

_____

_____

_____

_____

_____

_____

_____

_____

_____

_____

cc

CHAPTER SIX

My Next Step Is...

When I was in high school, I played on the golf team. I remember one occasion when we spent all day playing at a tournament and decided to stop for something to eat afterward at a fast-food Italian restaurant called Fazoli's.

It wasn't really about being in the mood for pasta. You see, they had a staff member whose sole responsibility was to walk around the restaurant and offer fresh, complimentary breadsticks. That's why we were there!

At some point during the meal, a challenge was offered by one of my teammates: whoever could eat the most breadsticks would win.

Win what, you may ask? Bragging rights, basically. Remember, we were in high school!

I should tell you I am highly competitive. I'll make a competition out of anything because it's fun for me. So as soon as we decided we were having a breadstick-eating competition, I had my game face on!

Thirty breadsticks later, I won that competition. But I also lost, if you know what I mean. (Please, don't judge me. We all made dumb decisions in high school.)

That night, I slept over at the house of one of my friends. The next morning, his mother came into the room to wake us up. When she opened the door, all I heard was her screaming.

"What did you guys do?" she yelled. We were still half asleep and had no idea what she was talking about.

"You smell so bad! This whole room reeks of garlic!" his mother continued, trying to keep from breathing in the breadstick-scented air.

My friend and I couldn't smell anything! We actually started arguing with her over whether the room smelled like garlic or not.

We've all had experiences like this, where we ended up smelling like something we ourselves could no longer smell. Everyone is aware that you smell—except you.

There's an important life-lesson here: *We have an amazing ability to adapt to our own stench.* This is why a person who has bad breath or body odor may be completely oblivious to it. And this concept plays out in other facets of our lives.

You may have a problem in your life right now you aren't even aware of, because you've adapted to the stench of that problem in your life. You've adjusted your routines to compensate for it, and you no longer notice its presence.

As a result, you may not be as spiritually healthy and as skilled at handling life as you should be, and you may need someone to lovingly step in and tell you there's something you need to pay attention to. This can happen to churches, too.

As we have established, it's ridiculously easy for us to look at other people, organizations, and systems and form opinions about what they need to change and how they can do things differently. Instead of looking at others, we need to look at ourselves and figure out how each of us can become a better "me" and contribute toward a better "we."

Being on the fence will clog your spiritual heart faster than a steady diet of doughnuts will clog your arteries. We need to be able to step back and evaluate ourselves and realize we might not smell nearly as good as we thought. And to do that, we need to make sure we are following Jesus.

How to Follow Jesus

Everyone has their own opinion on what it means to follow Jesus. That opinion is shaped by the people who have mentored us in our faith, the churches we have attended, and the various Christian resources we have read.

But with so many differing opinions out there, many of us aren't quite sure how to follow Jesus. We've taken a portion of what it means to follow Jesus and applied it to our entire relationship with Him.

When we have questions about something like this, it's important for us to go back to the Bible and see what God has to say on the matter. Let's take a look at a few verses that express what it means to follow Jesus.

Jesus replied, "I am the bread of life. Whoever comes to me will never be hungry again. Whoever believes in me will never be thirsty."

—John 6:35 (NLT)

Believing in Jesus and accepting Him as your Lord and Savior is a huge deal! But there's more, as seen in one of the most popular verses in the Bible:

For this is how God loved the world: He gave his one and only Son, so that everyone who believes in him will not perish but have eternal life.

—John 3:16 (NLT)

Some of us remember the moment or the season in our lives when we accepted Jesus as our Lord and Savior and became part of God's family. Whether we remember it clearly or not, it's the best decision we'll ever make. But again, that's not all there is to it. Simply put, Jesus doesn't *only* want to save you.

I'm not trying to demean or discredit salvation here. Salvation is a huge deal! But it is not the only part of following Jesus. Yes, He wants to save you, but He also wants to heal you. Beyond wanting to rescue you, He wants a relationship with you—to walk through life with you. He has more for you. Philippians 2:13 tells us, "For it is God who works in you to will and to act in order to fulfill his good purpose" (NIV).

God made you on purpose, for a purpose. He didn't rescue you and then tell you to sit in the corner and wait for heaven. The God of the universe wants a real, healthy, thriving relationship with you, not just an acknowledgment you believe He exists and that He did something amazing for you by saving you.

He knows you by name! He cares about you. It's more than a single transaction in one moment.

If you're looking for help with a problem, for wisdom, for strength, for peace, ask God. He wants to give you those things and more.

Faith Involves More Than Our Intellect

Many of us have relegated our relationship with Jesus to an intellectual exercise. We think it all boils down to the question of whether we are saved and what we believe.

Here's what Matt Chandler has to say about that: "To be a disciple of Jesus Christ means not that we believe some things intellectually, but that we have surrendered our lives over to His lordship ... we are following after Him. Anything less than that is not biblical Christianity—it's something of your imagination."[48]

Sounds harsh, doesn't it? But it is biblical. It is true. Let's take a look at a few verses here. Jesus said:

> *Anyone who wants to serve me must follow me, because my servants must be where I am. And the Father will honor anyone who serves me.*
> *—John 12:26 (NLT)*

Let that soak in for a moment. It's not just about intellectually believing God is real.

Jesus went into more detail in Matthew 16:24–25 (NLT):

> *Then Jesus said to his disciples, "If any of you wants to be my follower, you must give up your own way, take up your cross, and follow me. If you try to hang on to your life, you will lose it. But if you give up your life for my sake, you will save it."*

Jesus wants us to join Him, to follow Him. But to follow Jesus, we must give up our own way. This is Relationship 101. Anytime you are bonded to another person, whether it be through sports, dating, building a family, or leading a staff, you cannot have a thriving relationship if you abide by the old mantra, "My way or the highway."

I grew up playing sports and watched how our team bonded so much better when we gave up individual agendas of achieving great personal stats. When you get married, moments surface that put your differences on display—like folding towels. The law of staying happily married means one of you will need to start folding towels their way. When you raise kids, you'll want to sit and watch your favorite show, but so will your five-year-old—so, who gets their way? See, life is like this, but it's a good thing.

You and I don't build the best life when it's one hundred percent our way. This is especially true in our relationship with God. His way is always best. A relationship with Him is consistently submitted to His desire. It is a hard truth but a necessary one!

Following Jesus needs to go much, much further than an intellectual conversation. Many of us haven't allowed it to. We've let it stay in our brains without penetrating to our hearts. We've been satisfied with merely being religious.

If you've landed there, here's what I know about you: you are a good person, but you are struggling to find true peace in life. God wants better for you!

Take Your Next Step

Simply put, if you want to follow Jesus, you have to take your next step. There's always a next step, and there's always room for growth. This is true of any relationship.

Every relationship has a way for it to become stronger. Take a marriage relationship, for example. We tend to think it's only about changing your relationship status on your social media accounts, then getting engaged, and then getting married. But there's so much more to a deep, healthy marriage relationship!

Every relationship needs to be invested in, worked on, strengthened, and grown over time. There is no final destination here. Thinking a relationship doesn't have a next step is like thinking once you're at your peak level of physical fitness, you can stop working out and eat doughnuts for every meal. (Man, I talk about doughnuts a lot!)

And yet, sometimes we get so comfortable in the relationships that are important to us, we become complacent. We get lazy and put off investing in these relationships because we think there's always tomorrow. It happens all the time in marriages.

The Dangers of Complacency

Every March, my wife (Katy) and I celebrate another year of marriage. This is a big deal for us, and we're excited about every anniversary. Being in a marriage relationship is not easy. We're both human beings, and we both make mistakes.

Right now, our marriage is really good, but throughout the past eighteen years, we have experienced seasons when we've been complacent. We felt so comfortable with each other, we stopped working on our relationship.

We went from having regular dates and talking about how we were doing to watching our own movies on our own computers in silence. This wasn't an intentional decision. We found ourselves in seasons where we were busy or tired, and we gradually slid into complacency. We figured our spouse would be there tomorrow, so we stopped making each other a priority as we dealt with other things.

But our marriage relationship can be so much better and so much more fulfilling! That's what Katy and I want, not just a complacent coexistence where we live in the same home and raise our children to be functional adults.

The main reason we're still in love—shoot, the reason we believe our vows about death being the only thing that can end our marriage—is because we have both learned complacency is a threat. We have realized lazy marriages usually fail.

Whether it's a marriage relationship or another important relationship in our lives, we all crave relationships that are rich and fulfilling. But we aren't going to get there if we're complacent. There is always a next step to take. And it's the same with our relationship with God!

Get Fed

So, how do we get there? What's the next step we can take in our relationship with God, to get off the fence so it doesn't become stagnant and lukewarm? First Peter 2:2–3 (NLT) gives us some insight here:

> *Like newborn babies, you must crave pure spiritual milk so that you will grow into a full experience of salvation. Cry out for this nourishment, now that you have had a taste of the Lord's kindness.*

There's a maturing phase we go through. There are things we need to add to our lives to have a real and legitimate relationship with God when we truly follow Jesus. Peter told us the first step in following Jesus is getting fed.

All of us start life at the milk stage. We need other people to help us eat, and we're only capable of digesting liquids. You don't give a newborn a steak, right? Solid food is too much!

That's how it is when you're a new Christian. You show up at church each week to worship and learn and connect. Every time you attend, you learn something new.

When you start following Jesus, you need help. Don't feel bad about that. It straight-up says in 1 Peter 2:2–3, you need someone else to feed you!

I grew up in a pastor's family, and I have studied the Bible rigorously, both in an academic setting and on my own. And I can tell you I still need other people to feed me, to invest in me. It's okay to need others to help you understand the Bible and to remind you of what you already know to be true.

But let me offer you something I've learned while raising my kids. Eventually, your child is going to clamp their mouth shut and refuse to eat something you're trying to feed them. You're going to have to get creative to feed them because you can't feed them if their mouth isn't open.

If we are going to be spiritually fed, our heart needs to be open! Sometimes, we show up to church with the mindset that if it's not our favorite food being served, we're not going to eat it. We want to hear a specific worship song played or a sermon on a certain topic, or we're not going to engage with the service. We come with a demanding heart rather than an open heart.

I've worshiped God in environments I didn't prefer. I'll bet you have, too! And yet, He spoke to me in those environments—and even outside of church—because I had an open heart. An open heart feeds a hungry soul!

If you are a new Christian, a baby Christian, and you need others to feed you, make sure you come to the table with an open heart. A maturing Christian is one who is willing to eat whatever God puts on their plate, even if it's spinach!

Sunday Night Is On Your Own

Eventually, you will need to learn how to feed yourself. You will graduate to using your own fork and spoon.

There will come a day when, in addition to other people investing in you, you will be able to invest in yourself.

This is a big deal! Philippians 2:12 (NLT) states:

> *Dear friends, you always followed my instructions when I was with you. And now that I am away, it is even more important. Work hard to show the results of your salvation, obeying God with deep reverence and fear.*

Feeding yourself is hard work, but we have so many options to choose from. We have more access to biblical teaching about God than ever before in history. There is no reason for anyone to go spiritually hungry.

In our home, we have a tradition our kids absolutely hate. On Sunday nights, no one person makes dinner for the entire family. Dinner is up to the individual, and each person is responsible for making their own meal. We've been doing this for more than a decade, but every Sunday night, without fail, one of the kids—and it's a different one each week—will ask, "Hey, what's for dinner tonight?"

We'll ask, "Well, what did you do for dinner last Sunday night?" The answer is always the same: "I don't know."

Katy and I taught our kids how to cook. They know how to prepare meals for themselves. It's not that they've forgotten how to do these things. It's that they've gotten lazy. They don't feel like feeding themselves.

The lesson here is this: don't blame others for not fulfilling your responsibility to feed yourself. If your pastor's sermon isn't deep enough for you, the sermon isn't the problem. If the church you're attending isn't deep enough for you, the church isn't the problem.

If you can't find a single church that will finally deliver God's Word to you in the way you think it should be delivered, you may be trying to pass a responsibility on to other people that is actually meant for you.

If this describes you, please know I'm not condemning you. I simply want you to understand there's a fulfilling relationship with Jesus that can only happen when you take responsibility for feeding yourself and decide you are going to worship and study on your own. There comes a moment when we need to acknowledge it is not someone else's job to make sure we grow up.

Feed Others

One of the most telling, maturing transitions a human being goes through when helping themselves is to help others. Once you have learned how to feed yourself, it's crucial you and I embrace the opportunity we have to feed others. You can take what others have invested in you and what you have invested in yourself and start to serve other people. This is the place where so much fun in life begins to play out. There's a special joy in helping others know who Jesus is!

This is what Paul was talking about in Philippians 1:9–10 (NLT):

> *I pray that your love will overflow more and more, and that you will keep on growing in knowledge and understanding. For I want you to understand what really*

matters, so that you may live pure and blameless lives until the day of Christ's return.

God wants us to overflow with His love because others need help. Sometimes it might literally be providing a meal for someone. Other times, it might be helping a child understand who Jesus is or explaining the meaning of a Bible verse to a friend. There are so many opportunities for us to serve and invest in others.

If you feel like you're in a spiritual rut, the issue may be that you're not feeding others. Find a way you can serve someone in your life and see what happens. Take your next step.

What Are You Waiting For?

If you want an authentic relationship with Jesus—if you want to go from lukewarm, counterfeit Christianity to being a devoted follower of Jesus—now you know how to get off the fence.

Every relationship has a next step. That includes your relationship with God. No matter what stage you're at in your relationship with Him, He loves you too much to leave you there. He wants you to be fed! He wants you to learn how to feed yourself and how to feed others.

If you don't take that next step, you'll be settling for mere religion. You'll find yourself chasing after emotional experiences—worship music that moves you, teaching that makes you feel good about yourself—in hopes of filling the empty place where your authentic relationship with Jesus should be.

Let me save you a lot of time, energy, and heartache by telling you this: it doesn't work! Only relationship, not religion, will satisfy you.

Do you want to know the God you have been serving when you arrive in heaven? Then you have a next step. Maybe that next step is also your first step—accepting Jesus as your Lord and Savior and inviting Him into your life.

Your next step might be getting baptized into the faith, learning more about being part of the church, forgiving a hurt, or being generous with God by giving Him your time, talent, and treasure. Or it might be something else entirely.

So go ahead! Don't become lukewarm or complacent. Don't become oblivious to your own stench. Be brave and take your next step to get off the fence.

WORKBOOK

Chapter Six Questions

Question: When people look at you and your life, do you think they feel encouraged and inspired to follow Jesus? Or do you think they see a hypocrisy that is off-putting? Describe an example of hypocrisy from your own life. What can you learn from that experience?

_____

_____

_____

_____

_____

_____

_____

_____

DAVID KINNAN

Question: What are some of the specifics you have been taught about what it means to follow Jesus? How do those teachings line up with what God's Word says about following Jesus? Is there anything that has been added that's not in the Word, or anything that's in the Word but hasn't been included? How much of what it means to follow Jesus comes from 1) what has been taught to you, 2) what you learned from the Bible, and 3) your own opinions?

_____

_____

_____

_____

_____

_____

_____

_____

_____

_____

Question: Where do you think you fall in the develop-
ment of your faith? Are you at a place where you primarily
need others to feed you? Are you feeding yourself yet?
Are you at a place where you can feed others, too? What
is your next step toward developing a strong faith in God?
Do you need to seek out a small group? A mentor? Do you
need to start reading your Bible regularly?

_____

_____

_____

_____

_____

_____

_____

_____

_____

_____

Action: Evaluate where you're at in your relationship
with God. What has been your hesitation, or what com-
petes against your ability to remain consistent? Write a list
of all the choices you have to make throughout the day
that compete for your attention.

Now write out some next-step options for growing in your
relationship with God. Ask Him to show you the next step
you need to take to continue to grow in consistency. Then
take it!

Chapter Six Notes

CHAPTER SEVEN

This Is Real

As a kid, I have some memories that still sit in my brain with spooky clarity and detail. I once went to a haunted house with my family, and the experience has never left me. The clarity I have isn't about my age. I don't remember how old I was. I don't remember where this took place. Also, I don't remember why my parents thought the best use of the day was to take their young children to a haunted house. What I do have forever ingrained in my brain is a moment inside the haunted house.

My family and I were ushered into a room, a lobby of sorts. Once the door was closed, a very non-threatening individual began speaking through an intercom: "In a moment, we will open the door to begin your experience in the haunted house." I'm sure there were some more details laid out, but we were told we needed to wait for the previous group to finish. We waited. And waited. Without warning, the light went out. A room without windows is fine, unless someone removes the light. *"It's fine,"* I told myself.

Some comforting words were spoken over the intercom, "Folks, we apologize, but our power has gone out. We're working to remedy the situation. Please remain calm." Okay. It's all going to be fi— "Folks, just one thing to pay attention to: we recently scheduled an exterminator to come take care of a rodent problem. He is coming tomorrow. His advice is to stay away from any sign of the rats due to the likelihood of disease transmission."

"What? Rats?" Keep in mind, I was a kid. If an adult said it, I believed it.

The tension in the room was building. We were no longer waiting out a power issue. We were also trying to avoid disease-ridden rats. *"We're fine. We're fine, right?"*

"Wait—what was that on my foot? Someone must've bumped—wait ... that's not a foot." A scream filled the room. It wasn't me, don't worry. Another person yelled, "Rats!" I now felt them on my feet. *"Be brave, David. Be brave."* Another rat hit my foot!

"It's save-yourself time, now!" I found someone's back and jumped on them, my arms now wrapped around their neck, while I was climbing as high up their back as possible. I was in full-on scream mode, too. No, I hadn't hit puberty yet. Yes, my voice sounded like a squeaky, high-pitched girl in pain.

All of a sudden, *boom*, the lights flashed on. A door opened. I was in an awkward situation, as I realized I was nearly strangling my Aunt Marilyn and likely doing permanent damage to her back. I let go, now looking around confused. *"Where did the rats go? Are we safe? What just happened?"* It didn't take long to realize—nothing had really happened. It was all staged. That was the haunted house. It was all a game, a cheap way to dupe people like me into being terrified.

Nowadays, it's easy to find a haunted house or an escape room, just for the fun of it. While you participate, and as you grow up, you realize these places are fake. At any moment, you can bow out. But that's not how real life plays out. *Every day is real.* Decisions matter. People are affected by what we do and don't do.

Our relationship with Jesus shouldn't merely be an adrenaline rush or a way to find spirituality. Following Jesus is not only something that affects everything about our lives, but it dramatically impacts the lives of others as well. It's real and should be treated as reality, not fantasy.

Brennan Manning summed this up nicely when he said, "The greatest single cause of atheism in the world today is Christians, who acknowledge Jesus with their lips, then walk out the door, and deny Him by their lifestyle. That is what an unbelieving world simply finds unbelievable."[49]

That might seem like an extreme statement, but hypocrisy and lukewarm, counterfeit Christianity are a massive turnoff for people who have not yet joined God's family. Christians aren't perfect, but we should be—and can be—who we say we are. We should be off the fence. The only way to live out what we say is real is to address our daily decision-making and our daily thought process.

There's a Risk Involved

All of us have heard stories about heroes who have rescued other people. Sometimes it's a story from our own lives. Sometimes it's a story we read in the news. We value these stories because we know rescuing other people is a valuable endeavor.

Rescue requires sacrifice. This is why we have heroes. Even though we approve of rescuing others, not everyone is willing to make the sacrifice rescue requires.

In January 2020, a tragic avalanche occurred in Nepal. Seven people died, but thirty were rescued. An article from the *New York Times* described just how challenging it was to rescue these people: "Weather conditions were poor, with temperature dropping in the past two days, making the operation more difficult."[50]

This is in addition to the dangers of being in a mountain environment and all the snow from the avalanche. The rescuers sacrificed a lot even to organize this rescue operation. They took a huge risk, putting their lives on the line to save others.

The military likewise provides plenty of examples of heroism. One of the most common phrases used in stories about military rescues is "behind enemy lines." These courageous men and women venture into hostile territory to rescue total strangers, some of whom may support things they personally disagree with. They are willing to sacrifice, to put their own lives in danger, so others can have the opportunity for safety and a new life. It's absolutely incredible!

The last hero story: from 2019 to 2020, Australia experienced wildfires so severe, the entire world tuned in and offered help. At least thirty-three people died, and nearly three billion animals—yes, you read that correctly—died due to the fires or the loss of their habitat from the fires, or were otherwise displaced.[51]

People went out of their way to help the injured and displaced animals. A wildlife volunteer named Tracy Burgess hosted fifteen possums in her home! One of the possums had paws so severely burned, she had to change the bandages on them every night.[52]

You may draw the line at turning your house into a bed and breakfast for injured possums, but I think we can all agree that tending to the burned paws of a wounded wild animal involves a considerable amount of risk and sacrifice.

And therein lies the tension. *Rescue requires sacrifice.* When I think about my own life and watch those around me, I notice most people value sacrifice and the moments we witness it. However, the number of people advocating for sacrifice doesn't seem to match the number of those willing to sacrifice. Why? How do we get beyond only supporting sacrifice to actually living it out?

Simply put, when we treat each day with significance, we open up the option for sacrifice. Many of us are trying to live for God without living with faith. We're trying to have faith without faith. We want to be generous people, and display that attribute in our lives, but we're trying to figure out how to do it without sacrifice.

Don't let your mind play tricks on you: sacrifice isn't only a money conversation. When you talk about money, yes, you need to talk about sacrifice, but it's bigger than money. Forgiving someone is an act of sacrifice. It is the reason forgiveness should be treated like a gift.

Time is said to be even more valuable than our paychecks. Whom you give your time to, and how you spend your time, absolutely fall under the umbrella of sacrifice, which means it's risky. You can give someone time and they completely waste it. You can share legit wisdom with someone and they refuse it. Risk is risky.

Faith Isn't a Scheme

A few years ago, Katy and I were at the mall and there was a brand-new truck there. It was begging for me to own it! You could fill out a card to potentially win the truck, and I filled it out. I didn't think I had much chance of winning, but I had nothing to lose, so why not?

You can therefore imagine my surprise when I received a phone call from the people running the giveaway. They told me I was a finalist for the truck! I was so excited. I felt like I was winning at life—like all my hopes and dreams were coming true.

They invited me to come to a meeting where I would be given a key. If my key started the truck, I would be the winner. This felt like a mere formality, though. I was certain God wanted me to win it!

So Katy and I went to the meeting. They wanted us to sit down and listen to a presentation. I figured it was going to be about the truck—what its features were, what kind of maintenance it needed, and so forth. Instead, they started showing us pictures of vacation spots. I didn't want to waste their time, so I told them we weren't interested in purchasing a time share. I must've told them no at least thirty times—quite adamantly toward the end—before they gave up and told us we could go.

Wait a minute. What about the brand-new truck I was a finalist for?

They opened a drawer and pulled out a key. It didn't even go to the truck. It was just a key for a regular lock! I tried my key in the lock, and of course, it didn't work.

We went out to the parking lot to drive home in my not-brand-new truck, and I couldn't help but feel I had been duped. It was all a scheme to get me to buy a timeshare! They didn't want to give me anything; they just wanted to get something from me.

Unfortunately, churches and Christians can take the same approach. When a pastor preaches about sacrifice, it can feel like it's a money grab or a desperate plea for more of something. It's easy to feel like they want something from you. I can't stand that feeling—when the only reason someone said "hi" was because of what they wanted from me.

I hope you'll hear this about the topic of rescue and sacrifice. Before God asks anything of you, it's important to own what He's done for you. It's not a scheme. It's a relationship. If you have never allowed God into your life and have never received His salvation, His forgiveness, and His love, He is not asking you to give to Him. God won't ask you for money you don't have, time you don't have, or resources you don't have, but He will look at the money, time, resources, and gifts He entrusted you with as an opportunity for faith and rescue missions. *But first,* He wants you to receive what He has to give you!

If God had not dealt with our sin problem through the sacrifice of His Son, all of us would be facing eternal damnation. Hell. No exceptions, no exclusions. I'm not perfect, and you aren't perfect. Not one of us measures up to God's standard of holy perfection apart from the blood of Christ. Do not oversimplify or disregard the magnitude of what God sacrificed in order to rescue us!

Portion Control and Sacrifice

Why, then, does God ask us to give after we have received? Why doesn't He just continue to give to us without asking for anything in return? It's because He knows sacrifice will transform our hearts.

Let's look at Philemon 1:6: "And I am praying that you will put into action the generosity that comes from your faith as you understand and experience all the good things we have in Christ" (NLT). In other words, to experience all the good things we have in Christ, we need to put sacrifice into action. The way of Jesus is a sacrificial way of life. It's important to note, God is constantly using whatever we'll sacrifice as a tool to help someone know what you know: how much God loves them.

I have mentioned my health "journey" multiple times, but there is a major lesson I need to share with you. It's about portions. I grew up without ever giving attention to healthy portions in relation to food. Throughout high school, if it sounded good, I ate it. Throughout the first forty years of my life, I ate whatever was put in front of me. I would rationalize it by considering it a way to honor those who prepared the food, or I would think about how leaving food on my plate would be wasteful.

For most of my life, I've had an unhealthy relationship with food. I've used it for more than fuel. It was a tool for celebration. It was also a tool for consoling sadness or anger. I am a foodie. I enjoy new restaurants, new flavors, new recipes. I follow the hashtag *#bbq* on Instagram.

However, covered in an acceptable behavior of "enjoying food," God wanted to help me get healthier, and not merely physically. Mostly, I believe, He wanted my spiritual heart to get some attention.

I began a portion-control plan with eating, and it changed how I treated food. I learned my eyes underestimate what I put on my plate. I learned my expectations of how much food I required were completely off. For a season, I learned how to use a food scale to measure protein. I used measuring cups to make sure my servings were appropriate. After a few months, my body shed seventy-five pounds.

Putting in a book what I just told you is freakishly scary. What if I fall off the wagon? It's a risk, isn't it?

Portioning is a topic all throughout the Bible, if you pay attention. Here's some examples:

> *The LORD God placed the man in the Garden of Eden to tend and watch over it. But the Lord God warned him, "You may freely eat the fruit of every tree in the garden—except the tree of the knowledge of good and evil. If you eat its fruit, you are sure to die."*
> **—Genesis 2:15–17** *(NLT)*

Eat from anywhere *except*—that's portion talk

> Then the LORD said to Moses, "Look, I'm going to rain down
> food from heaven for you. Each day the people can go out
> and pick up as much food as they need for that day. I will
> test them in this to see whether or not they will follow my
> instructions.
> —*Exodus 16:4* (NLT)

Gather only as much as you need for *one day*—that's
portion talk.

> When you harvest the crops of your land, do not harvest
> the grain along the edges of your fields, and do not pick up
> what the harvesters drop. Leave it for the poor and the for-
> eigners living among you. I am the LORD your God.
> —*Leviticus 23:22* (NLT)

Leave a section of crops for the poor and foreigners—
that's portion talk.

> Jesus sat down near the collection box in the Temple and
> watched as the crowds dropped in their money. Many rich
> people put in large amounts. Then a poor widow came and
> dropped in two small coins.
>
> Jesus called his disciples to him and said, "I tell you the
> truth, this poor widow has given more than all the others
> who are making contributions. For they gave a tiny part of
> their surplus, but she, poor as she is, has given everything
> she had to live on."
> —*Mark 12:41–44* (NLT)

Jesus compared the portions of money given to God—that's portion talk.

God has always wanted us to see a connection between the three parts of our lives: provision, portion, and worship. Just look at the example Jesus gave us when teaching us how to pray: "Give us today the food we need." Matthew 6:11 (NLT) That's a call to live a life including portion control—and portion control requires a willingness to risk and sacrifice.

One crucial change in my life is how I focus on a food scale rather than a bodyweight scale. The latter tells me the results of weekly and monthly decisions. The food scale is a portion approach to daily choices with long-term benefits. I believe God has called us to the same way of living, and it's not just about food.

On that note, it's time for an activity. I want you to make a fist. Clench it as tightly as you can. Do this for thirty seconds. Don't cheat. After thirty seconds, open your fist. Most of us feel the tension in our hand now, and our forearm has definitely been woken up. Closing your fist tightly for an extended amount of time doesn't just wear out your fingers. Everything in your arm is affected.

Many of us take a closed-fist approach to our resources we have and want in our lives. We are holding onto them so tightly, no one can take them away from us. We think of ourselves as being our own planners, protectors, and providers, so we refuse to let go of what we have earned or what we have. In essence, we refuse to let go of a portion because we believe it's all for us.

But what happens when we open up our hands? This approach acknowledges it is God's job to provide for us and protect us, and everything we have belongs to Him. It seems like a risky way to live, but it is worth it! It's portion control.

At what point did we start assuming things belong to us? We are merely stewards. Whether we have a lot or a little, it all belongs to God.

Taking a closed-fist approach to life means we are always in a fighting posture. You may not have ever had aspirations to become a champion boxer, but many of us have indeed become skilled at living life in a fighter's posture. We are always ready to defend what we erroneously believe to be ours. We worked hard for it and provided it for ourselves, and there is no way we're going to let anyone else have any of it—right?

A scarcity mentality takes over, and we feel like we don't have enough. We find ourselves fighting God or our pastor or our church because we don't want them to take it away from us. Do you know how difficult it is to be a Christian and live this way? You can't love others from this kind of emotional and spiritual posture!

But when you take an open-handed approach to sacrifice, you are in a posture where you genuinely care about others. You're living your life from a helpful, loving emotional and spiritual posture.

And not only are your hands open to give; they're also open to receive. You cannot receive joy, fulfillment, and purpose from God if your hands are clinging tightly to all the things that are "yours."

Whatever you hold back from God will hold you back. This applies to all of us, and yes, it requires faith. If you withhold your marriage from God, then your marriage is going to hold you back. You may have given everything else in your life over to God, but if you don't allow Him to touch your marriage, it will hold you back.

The same goes for your career, your thought life, and your emotional hurts. Whatever you hold onto most usually ends up having a hold on you.

Sacrifice turbocharges your relationship with God and transforms your heart. If you let go of what you are holding and hold onto Him instead, I promise you, you will experience God holding onto you!

The Fuel for Rescue Missions

In addition to transforming your heart, sacrifice fuels rescue missions. Philemon 1:7 says, "Your love has given me much joy and comfort, my brother, for your kindness has often refreshed the hearts of God's people."

This verse reveals the fruit of sacrifice—joy, comfort, refreshment. Sacrifice makes an impact in people's lives and changes them for the better.

Proverbs 11:10 tells us, "The whole city celebrates when the godly succeed; they shout for joy when the wicked die" (NLT). It might seem a little implausible to you that an entire city would celebrate someone's achievements, but that is exactly what happens when a football team makes it to the Super Bowl or a baseball team makes it to the World Series. For a sports team to get all the way to a championship game is an amazing accomplishment. Many people don't get to see their favorite team get that far in their lifetime, so when it happens, it's incredible.

Interestingly, you don't really see the fans of the teams that lost the opportunity congratulating the fans of the teams going to the championship. It's not easy to celebrate what goes on in the lives of other people when we feel we are missing out, is it?

Going back to Proverbs 11:10, it's important to note that the city celebrates when the "godly" succeed. This isn't about sports or accolades or money. It's about people who love and honor God, experiencing success.

And what is success for a godly person? It's when someone finds the hope of Jesus Christ and accepts Him as their Lord and Savior. It's when that person continues to grow in their relationship with Jesus and mature in their faith. That's what should be considered success to a Christian!

When the godly succeed, someone goes to heaven. When the godly succeed, someone in need is provided for. Success is taking care of the spiritual and physical needs of others. And that's why a whole city can celebrate when a Jesus-following church embraces the sacrificial approach to life Jesus modeled, which also enables rescue missions.

If churches in your city were ever to close their doors, the city should be devastated because it would mean people aren't being taken care of spiritually or physically.

Your Lifestyle Should Reflect Your Faith

Many of us struggle to *believe* the truth of God because we don't *apply* the truth of God. Instead of living out our faith, we deny Him with our lifestyles. We deny He is real. We deny He provides.

I don't say these things to condemn you or make you feel guilty. I say them to encourage you to grow. If you are a follower of Jesus Christ and you have not been sacrificing for God, if you have been afraid He isn't trustworthy, then let this be the moment God intervenes in your life. Let this be the moment He feeds you nourishment you desperately need and helps you to move forward recognizing the very real impact of your choices.

You can easily bring back the "get away from zero" approach here. I teach people a process when it comes to sacrifice:

- Move from nothing to something, then
- Move from something to scheduled, and then
- Move from scheduled to sacrificial.

The important part: keep growing. Remember, your church cannot reach out to others and address their spiritual and physical needs if you refuse to sacrifice regularly.

Everyone Deserves to Be Rescued

Take a moment to think of the most important person in your life. Imagine they find themselves in a desperate situation and need to be rescued immediately.

Would you want emergency personnel to make excuses instead of rushing out to help them? Of course not!

You would want them to be rescued as soon as possible. You would even race to their rescue yourself.

Everyone is important to God. Everyone matters, so sacrifice matters. I need you to help me reach the people in my life who won't listen to me, and you need me to help reach the people in your life who won't listen to you.

We need each other. We need to sacrifice for each other because God has been sacrificial for us, and we need to be sacrificial for God. Living this way will help each of us to become a better "me." And not only will that lead to a better church overall; it will also draw others to come be a part of the body of Christ.

Never let the fear of commitment or concern about scarcity stop you from a life of sacrifice! And never let your limited resources keep you from getting a transformed heart and participating in rescue missions.

Chapter Seven Questions

Question: Have you ever risked something for the sake of helping someone else? What was the result of taking that risk?

_____

_____

_____

_____

_____

_____

_____

_____

_____

_____

_____

Question: How has God sacrificed for you? How does thinking about the blessings God has given you impact how you want to be toward others? What things in your life do you need to let go of so God can fully pour into your life?

_____

_____

_____

_____

_____

_____

_____

_____

_____

_____

Question: Looking at your life from the categories of time, talent, and treasure, how would you rate what you're giving to God? Zero? A full 100? What category is the toughest for you? Why? Which is the easiest? Why?

_____

_____

_____

_____

_____

_____

_____

_____

_____

_____

_____

_____

Action: Ask God to show you someone in your life who needs rescuing. How can you take a risk and reach out to them?

Chapter Seven Notes

CONCLUSION

A Better You

As much as we might like to point fingers at others, change begins with the individual. There is no way for any group we are a part of—whether it's our family, our workplace, or our church—to become a better "we" unless each of us does the hard work of becoming a better "me."

It all starts with a full cardiac workup—making sure we have a clean and healthy spiritual heart. It's impossible for us to live the full life Jesus has for us if our spiritual hearts are clogged with sin, bitterness, selfishness, greed, and perpetual outrage.

A healthy spiritual heart overflows with unconditional love, irrational generosity, and a sense of unwavering mission. Just like the father in the Parable of the Prodigal Son, we are committed to making love personal and loving people even when they behave in ways that are unlovable.

We are committed to extending generosity to people even if they haven't shown they deserve it. We are committed to the roles God has given us in life and to living by His convictions rather than our own preferences.

But it doesn't end there! A healthy spiritual heart will not remain healthy for long if we're counterfeit Christians with a lukewarm faith in God. We should instead aspire to be Christians who are off the fence of apathy and have an authentic, biblically sound relationship with Jesus.

This begins when we take responsibility for our relationship with God by showing up for Him and for other people. Instead of keeping our hope in Christ to ourselves, we need to share it with others by sharing our story and inviting them into our lives.

As we continue to follow Jesus, we must keep our hearts open to receive His teaching and learn how to be fed, how to feed ourselves, and how to feed other people. This all culminates in us being equipped to rescue others as we engage in sacrificial generosity.

It is my hope that after reading this book and working through the workbook sections, you are well on your way to becoming a better "me" and contributing to every group you are a part of making it a better "we."

May you continue to experience the fruits of taking responsibility for your own heart, your own life, and your own faith. And may you see your relationship with God and your relationships with other people flourish!

REFERENCES

Notes

1. Weigel, Moira. "Pajama Rich." Real Life. https://reallifemag.com/pajama-rich/.

2. John Hopkins Medicine. "Heart Disease." https://www.hopkins medicine.org/endoscopic-weight-loss-program/conditions/heart_disease.html.

3. Barclay, William. *The Gospel of Luke.* Presbyterian Publishing Corporation, 2017.

4. Wax, Trevin. "Prodigal Son 9: The Running Father." The Gospel Coalition. https://www.thegospelcoalition.org/blogs/trevin-wax/prod igal-son-9-the-running-father/.

5. Spitzer, Robert J. "Who Is God?" Magis Center of Reason and Faith. https://docs.google.com/viewerng/viewer?url=https://magis center.com/wp-content/uploads/2017/07/Who_is_God.pdf&hl=en.

6. Spitzer, "Who Is God?"

7. Linsley, Alice C. "The Fatted Calf." Biblical Anthropology. May 30, 2015. http://biblicalanthropology.blogspot.com/2015/05/the-

fatted-calf.html.

8. Brown, Brené. *The Gifts of Imperfection: Let Go of Who You Think You're Supposed to Be and Embrace Who You Are.* Hazelden Publishing, 2010, p. 83.

9. *Bible Study Tools,* "epithumeo." https://www.biblestudytools.com /lexicons/greek/nas/epithumeo.html.

10. *Bible Study Tools,* "epithumia." https://www.biblestudytools. com/lexicons/greek/kjv/epithumia.html.

11. Pletcher, Kenneth. "Dead Sea." *Encyclopædia Britannica.* https:// www.britannica.com/place/Dead-Sea.

12. Earth Observatory. "Saltiest Pond on Earth." https://earth observatory.nasa.gov/images/84955/saltiest-pond-on-earth.

13. Dead Sea. "What Is the Dead Sea? Where Is the Dead Sea Located?" https://www.deadsea.com/articles-tips/interesting-facts/ why-is-the-dead-sea-called-the-dead-sea/#name.

14. Nonprofits Source. "Church and Religious Charitable Giving Statistics." https://nonprofitssource.com/online-giving-statistics/ church-giving/.

15. Wang, Amy B. "Flooding Trapped Workers at a Mexican Bakery for Two Days. They Spent It Baking for Harvey Victims." *The Washington Post.* August 31, 2017. https://www.washingtonpost. com/news/inspired-life/wp/2017/08/31/flooding-trapped-these- mexican-bakers-for-two-days-they-spent-it-baking-for-harvey- victims/.

16. Bennett, Bill. *The American Patriot's Almanac.* Thomas Nelson, 2008, p. 408.

17. *Lexico,* "waver." https://www.lexico.com/en/definition/waver.

18. *Merriam Webster Dictionary,* "waver." https://www.merriam-webster.com/dictionary/waver.

19. Gibbs, David C. "Conviction Versus Preference." Testimony Press. https://www.testimonypress.org/wp-content/uploads/2015/11/conviction_vs_preference.pdf.

20. Batterson, Mark. "Are You All In?" Charisma, 2013. https://www.charismamag.com/spirit/spiritual-growth/18291-are-you-all-in.

21. Batterson, "Are You All In?"

22. Zavada, Jack. "Meet Simon the Zealot: A Mystery Apostle." Learn Religions. July 17, 2018. https://www.learnreligions.com/simon-the-zealot-mystery-apostle-701071.

23. *Encyclopaedia Britannica.* "St. Matthew." https://www.britannica.com/biography/Saint-Matthew.

24. Blackaby, R., C. V. King, H. T. Blackaby. *Experiencing God: Knowing and Doing the Will of God.* Revised and expanded edition. Broadman & Holman Publishers, 2008, p. 32.

25. Blackaby, King, and Blackaby, *Experiencing God.*

26. Blackaby, King, and Blackaby, *Experiencing God,* p. 69.

27. *Dictionary.com,* "drift." https://www.dictionary.com/browse/drift.

28. Bork, Paul F. "What Hierapolis Tells Us About Laodicea: On Biblical Archeology." 1977. https://www.ministrymagazine.org/archive/1977/08/what-hierapolis-tells-us-about-laodicea.

29. Duvall, J. S. *Revelation. Teach the Text Commentary Series.* Baker Publishing Group, 2014.

30. Bible Tools. "What the Bible Says About Laodicea." https://www. bibletools.org/index.cfm/fuseaction/topical.show/RTD/cgg/ID/248/ Laodicea.htm.

31. NeverThirsty. "Laodicea—the Lukewarm Church Is Neither Hot Nor Cold." https://www.neverthirsty.org/bible-studies/evaluating-health-your-church/the-lukewarm-church-is-neither-hot-nor-cold/.

32. Kinnaman, David, Mark Matlock, and Aly Hawkins. *Faith for Exiles: 5 Ways for a New Generation to Follow Jesus in Digital Babylon.* Baker Publishing Group, 2019.

33. Enduring World. "1 Samuel 31—the Death of Saul and His Sons." https://enduringword.com/bible-commentary/1-samuel-31/.

34. Guzik, David. "Study Guide for 2 Samuel 9." Blue Letter Bible. https://www.blueletterbible.org/Comm/guzik_david/StudyGuide201 7-2Sa/2Sa-9.cfm?a=276001.

35. Henry, Matthew. *Matthew Henry's Commentary on the Whole Bible: Complete and Unabridged.* Hendrickson Publishers, 2008.

36. Guzik, "Study Guide for 2 Samuel 9."

37. Smith, Chuck. "C-2000 Commentary." https://calvarychapel.com /pastorchuck/c2k.

38. Guzik, "Study Guide for 2 Samuel 9."

39. Bayes, Ros. "A Biblical View of Disability." https://www.bethink ing.org/human-life/a-biblical-view-of-disability.

40. Smith, "C-2000 Commentary."

41. Kurth, Ricky. "Dining with the King." Berean Bible Society. https://www.bereanbiblesociety.org/dining-with-the-king/.

42. Noble, D. L. "A Legacy: The United States Life-Saving Service."

U.S. Life-Saving Service Heritage Association. https://uslife-savingservice.org/wp-content/uploads/A-History-of-the-USLSS-Denis-Noble.pdf.

43. National Park Service. "US Life-Saving Service." https://www.nps.gov/articles/life-saving-service.htm.

44. National Park Service. "Physical History." https://www.nps.gov/goga/learn/historyculture/upload/Physical%20History%20Part%201-3.pdf.

45. U.S. Life-Saving Service Heritage Association. "'You Have to Go Out, But Your Don't Have to Come Back' The United States Life-Saving Service." https://uslife-savingservice.org/wp-content/uploads/The-United-States-Life-Saving-Service-in-Lewes.pdf.

46. U.S. Life-Saving Service Heritage Association. "Home." https://uslife-savingservice.org/.

47. U.S. Life-Saving Service Heritage Association. "Previous Annual Conference Locations." https://uslife-savingservice.org/annual-conference/past-annual-conferences/.

48. Chandler, Matt. "Sermons – Matt Chandler – Biblically Serious." The Village Church Resources, May 6, 2019. YouTube video. https://www.youtube.com/watch?v=RhVw-PRB4v8.

49. Simpson, Ben. "The Ragamuffin Legacy." Relevant Magazine. April 16, 2013. https://www.relevantmagazine.com/faith/ragamuffin-legacy/.

50. The Associated Press. "Avalanche in Nepal Leave at Least 7 Missing." The New York Times. January 18, 2020. https://www.nytimes.com/2020/01/18/world/asia/nepal-avalanche.html.

51. BBC News. "Australia's Fires 'Killed or Harmed Three Billion

Animals.'" July 28, 2020. https://www.bbc.com/news/world-australia-53549936#:~:text=Nearly%20three%20billion%20animals%20were,)%2C%20which%20commissioned%20the%20report.

52. CBC Radio. "What It's Like Working with Wildlife Rescued from Australia's Deadly Fires." January 3, 2020. https://www.cbc.ca/aradi o/asithappens/as-it-happens-friday-edition-1.5414075/what-it-s-like-working-with-wildlife-rescued-from-australia-s-deadly-fires-1.5414 082.

About the Author

David Kinnan is the lead pastor of Fountain Springs Church. This church that nearly closed its doors forever has been listed as one of the nation's one hundred fastest-growing churches multiple times. Now a church with multiple locations, FSC lives for one mission: "Show people who Jesus is." David and Katy have been married eighteen years and enjoy raising their four children in the beautiful Black Hills of South Dakota. Follow him on Instagram @davidkinnan and Facebook @kinnandavid.